Guide to the Tarot

LUCEM LIBRIS
DISSEMINAMUS

**GEDDES &
GROSSET**

Published 2001 by Geddes & Grosset, an imprint of
Children's Leisure Products Limited

© 1996 Children's Leisure Products Limited,
David Dale House, New Lanark ML11 9DJ, Scotland

First published 1996, reprinted 2001

ISBN 1 85534 388 6

Printed and bound in the UK

Contents

Introduction

The exact origins of Tarot are unknown. It seems that the earliest records of its existence show that it was first known as a card game with the French title *Les Tarots*, which was played in Italy. This game, still played today in some countries, bears no resemblance to the current practice of using Tarot cards for the purpose of divination.

The Tarot pack was used solely in card games for some considerable time. It was not until the late eighteenth century that it seems to have become connected with the practice of divination. Nowadays Tarot cards are used mainly by people who are trying to predict the future, although they are also sometimes used as an object of focus by people who are practising meditation.

A great many theories exist as to the origins of Tarot cards, linking them to different cultures and beliefs. One of these theories is that Tarot originated from Egyptian hieroglyphics. The connection between Tarot and the Egyptian culture was explored by a French intellectual of the eighteenth century, Court de Gebelin. While working on a vast study of the occult, he developed the theory that there existed a link between Tarot and 'the Book of

Thoth', Thoth being the Egyptian god of science. Trismegistus, a Greek alchemist and teacher of magic, is supposed to have set down his teachings in this 'book'. The popularity of this theory can be accounted for by the great interest in all things Egyptian at the time.

In the mid-nineteenth century the work of Court de Gebelin was developed by Alphonse Louis Constant, another Frenchman with an interest in the occult. He developed a system for interpreting Tarot cards that inspired the printing of several Tarot decks, including the most popular Tarot deck, the Rider-Waite deck, which is used to form the illustrations in this book.

Another theory concerning the origins of the Tarot cards is that the Knights Templar set down their beliefs in the twenty-two cards of the Major Arcana. It is held that this was done just before the dissolution of the Knights Templar and the execution of the Grand Master, Jacques du Molay, in 1314. Although there are several Christian elements in Tarot cards, any connection between the Knights Templar and the introduction of Tarot cards is thought to be unlikely.

Other suggestions regarding the origins of Tarot are that it was brought to Europe from Asia by gypsies, that it is of Arabic origin and crusaders brought it back with them, or that it is of Indian origin and a very early form of chess. There do seem to be very close connections between the Tarot and the Cabbala, which is an ancient

Jewish practice of mysticism and magic. The mystery of the origins adds to the magic and individual interpretation of the cards today.

Whatever the true origin, Tarot as we know it today, has its root in the early Renaissance period of history. The earliest surviving Tarot cards are Italian and were made for the Visconti family in Milan around the year 1450. These are sometimes known as the Bembo cards after the artist, Bonifacio Bembo, who is usually credited with painting them for the Visconti family. Not everyone believes that Bembo was the person who was responsible for the making of the cards, and some people ascribe their creation to Francesco Zavattari.

Many of the cards that are regarded as being historical and genuine are French, not Italian, in their design. Of these, the Tarot de Marseilles is well known. In the seventeenth century the manufacture of Tarot cards in northern Italy more or less stopped. Cards were then imported into Italy from France.

Tarot cards have altered and developed over the centuries. The Rider-Waite pack is not exactly the same as the Tarot de Marseilles, and in turn the Tarot de Marseilles is not the same the Visconti pack. Some of the earliest packs had more than seventy-eight cards, and the order of the cards has changed several times.

In the late twentieth century Tarot became widely popular as people became fascinated by New Age practices and a desire to know what the future holds in these uncertain times. Once, those interested in the occult were regarded with suspicion, but now the production of occult books and decks of Tarot cards is big business. There are a great many sets of Tarot cards to choose from – even Salvador Dali produced a Tarot pack as one of his works. The decks that exist vary in their symbolism. Some draw inspiration from ancient civilisations, such as that of the Celts, and some are based on fantasy. All the packs that exist are beautifully designed and can be appreciated as works of art in their own right. Indeed, a great many of the Tarot decks that are sold will never be used for the purpose of divination.

There is often quite a lot of mystique and ritual relating to the use of Tarot cards, perhaps because of the great amount of ancient symbolism attached to them. Many users of Tarot cards feel that they must keep their cards wrapped in a piece of black or purple silk, and many then place the silk-wrapped pack in a home-made wooden box.

Some believe that a Tarot pack should never be bought by the person who is going to use it. They feel that to have maximum effectiveness a Tarot pack should be purchased by someone else and given to the intended user as a gift.

Many users of Tarot do not like people other than themselves or their clients touching their cards. They feel that they have built up a special symbolic relationship with their cards which will be destroyed by someone else's touch.

Several users of Tarot like to observe certain rituals when they are giving a reading. They may like, for example, to burn incense or play music. Others may open a reading by saying a prayer. Some may feel that they have to be in a particular part of the room, facing in a particular direction.

A Tarot pack consists of 78 cards altogether, 22 of which form the Major Arcana. The Major Arcana cards are more significant than the cards of the Minor Arcana as they symbolise major changes in the querent's life. Each card has a number, and this is also significant when doing a reading as the recurrence of a particular number in a reading has its own significance. The numbers are:

Fool	0	Justice	11
Magician	1	Hanged Man	12
High Priestess	2	Death	13
Empress	3	Temperance	14
Emperor	4	Devil	15
Hierophant	5	Tower	16
Lovers	6	Star	17
Chariot	7	Moon	18
Strength	8	Sun	19
Hermit	9	Judgment	20
Wheel	10	World	21

The other 56 cards form the Minor Arcana and are split into four suits: Wands (sometimes referred to as Sceptres, Rods, Batons or Staves), Cups, Swords and Pentacles (sometimes referred to as Coins or Discs). Each suit has ten numbered cards (for example, the Eight of Pentacles) and four court cards. The court cards are the Page, the Knight, the Queen and the King.

The Minor Arcana cards are said to have associations with today's playing cards, and those interested in the art of cartomancy may find that there are similarities in the interpretations of cards. Below are the suits of playing cards and their suggested antecedents:

Wands	Diamonds
Cups	Hearts
Swords	Clubs
Pentacles	Spades

Each suit of the Minor Arcana has its own significance and symbolism. Minor Arcana cards symbolise the thoughts, feelings, actions and desires that allow changes to occur in the querent's life. The numbered Minor Arcana cards can be dominated by the court cards and the Major Arcana cards, so their interpretation will be influenced by the other cards in the reading. The interpretation of a reading will also be influenced if one suit is strongly represented. For example, if in a Celtic Cross spread three of the cards were from the suit of Cups it would indicate the prominence of the querent's emotional circumstances.

Wands

Wands are associated with thoughts, inspirations, desires and the identifying of goals. Although other terms exist, Wands is the most favoured as it captures the sense of magic and spiritual power associated with the suit. Wands indicate that the querent has ambitions and thoughts that may create change in the future.

Cups

Cups are associated with emotions, feelings and spiritual experiences. Cups indicate that the querent will be preoccupied with relationships and spiritual experiences. There is a focus on being rather than on doing.

Swords

Swords are associated with action, conflict and struggle. Swords indicate that the querent will be involved in arguments and disputes, and although this may at first appear to be negative it can be very positive. Swords can indicate that stagnant situations will change and ill feeling be brought out into the open.

Pentacles

Pentacles are associated with the realisation of goals, material wellbeing and rewards for hard work. Pentacles indicate a prosperous time for the querent, but it is important to remember that material wellbeing and spiritual health do not always go hand in hand.

Using Tarot Cards

Choosing a Tarot Deck

When buying a deck of Tarot cards it is important to look at all the different types of cards that exist and to study them. The individual should choose a deck that he or she is attracted to and appreciates.

Storing Tarot Cards

Some people believe that the way in which Tarot cards are stored is very important. Experienced users often keep their decks wrapped in black or purple silk and placed in a box so that the power of the cards' energies will not be altered or weakened. Experienced divinators will often not let others touch their decks or will ensure that this is kept to a minimum. If you go to a professional Tarot reader, you will probably be allowed only to cut the deck and will not be asked to shuffle the cards. This practice keeps the individual bond between the divinator and his or her pack, which allows for intuitive interpretations of readings.

First Steps in the Practice of Divination

1. On purchasing a deck of cards, the querent should

hold each card and familiarise himself or herself with the card and its interpretations. The bond will grow stronger with time, and more intuitive interpretations will be the result.

2. Before beginning a reading, the querent should formulate the question he or she wishes to ask and repeat it aloud.

3. While shuffling the cards the querent should meditate on the question being asked but think of nothing else.

4. The querent and divinator should not allow personal bias and preconceived ideas to enter the mind during the process.

The Significator

The first step is to select a significator card, which represents the person making the query (the querent) or the matter about which the inquiry is being made. The court cards of the Minor Arcana are the cards to choose from to act as significators:

King of Wands a fair-haired or auburn-haired man over forty years of age with blue eyes and a fair complexion.
Queen of Wands a fair-haired or auburn-haired woman over forty years of age with blue eyes and a fair complexion.

Knight of Wands a fair-haired or auburn-haired man under forty years of age with blue eyes and a fair complexion.

Page of Wands a fair-haired or auburn-haired woman under forty years of age with blue eyes and a fair complexion.

King of Cups a man over forty years of age with light brown hair and grey or blue eyes.

Queen of Cups a woman over forty years of age with light brown hair and grey or blue eyes.

Knight of Cups a man under forty years of age with light brown hair and grey or blue eyes.

Page of Cups a woman under forty years of age with light brown hair and grey or blue eyes.

King of Swords a dark-haired man over forty years of age with hazel or grey eyes and a dull complexion.

Queen of Cups a dark-haired woman over forty years of age with hazel or grey eyes and a dull complexion.

Knight of Cups a dark-haired man under forty years of age with hazel or grey eyes and a dull complexion.

Page of Cups a dark-haired woman under forty years of age with hazel or grey eyes and a dull complexion.

King of Pentacles a swarthy-skinned man over forty years of age with very dark hair and eyes.

Queen of Pentacles a swarthy-skinned woman over forty years of age with very dark hair and eyes.

Knight of Pentacles a swarthy-skinned man under forty years of age with very dark hair and eyes.

Page of Pentacles a swarthy-skinned woman under forty years of age with very dark hair and eyes.

The above significators are based on physical attributes alone, and if these do not seem appropriate it is possible for the person doing the reading to choose a more suitable card based on character traits. It is also possible that the significator card can reflect the nature of the inquiry. For example, if the querent wants to know if a legal action is likely, the Justice card of the Major Arcana could be used as the significator.

The Celtic Spread

The significator having been selected, it should be placed on the table facing upwards. The significator card will be under card number one in the diagram.

The querent should then shuffle and cut the rest of the pack three times, keeping the cards facing down and meditating on the inquiry that is being made.

Then the querent should turn over the first card of the pack and lay this card over the significator. This card is card number 1 in the diagram on page 21. This card should be interpreted as signifying the influences affecting the querent and the general atmosphere.

Then the querent should turn over the second card in the pack and lay it across card number 1. This card should be interpreted as symbolising the nature of the obstacles that stand in the way of the querent.

The querent should then turn over the third card and place it in the position above cards number 1 and 2. This card should be interpreted as representing the querent's aim or ideal in relation to the inquiry or the best that can be achieved under the circumstances but that has not yet happened.

The querent should then turn over the fourth card and place it in the position below cards number 1 and 2. This card should be interpreted as representing the foundation or basis of the matter, that which has already happened.

The querent should then turn over the fifth card and place it to the right of cards number 1 and 2. This card should be interpreted as representing that which is happening or has just happened.

The querent should then turn over the sixth card and place it to the left of cards number 1 and 2. This card should be interpreted as representing the future and that which is ahead of the querent.

These cards are now positioned in the shape of a cross, and the following four cards should be placed in a line from bottom to top to the right of the cross formation.

The querent should then turn over the seventh card and place it at the bottom of the line to the right of the cross. This card should be interpreted as representing the position or attitude of the querent in the circumstances.

The querent should then turn over the eighth card and

place it above card number 7. This card should be interpreted as signifying the environment and influences of the querent.

The querent should then turn over the ninth card and place it above card number 8. This card should be interpreted as identifying the querent's hopes and fears.

Finally, the querent should turn over the tenth card and place this above card number 9. This card should be interpreted as representing the final result, the culmination that is brought about by the influences of the other cards in the reading.

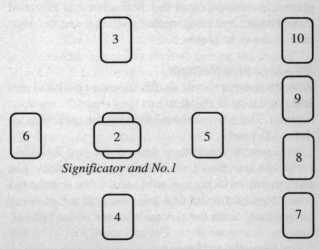

Significator and No.1

The spread is now complete, but should card number 10 be a difficult card to draw a final decision from, or if it does not have any obvious association with the inquiry, it would be wise to repeat the reading using the tenth card as the significator instead of the one previously used. In this case the pack must again be shuffled and cut three times before the ten cards can be laid out as before.

If the tenth card is a court card, it indicates that the matter of the inquiry rests in the hands of the character represented by the court card. It is possible to achieve a greater understanding of the motivation and nature of this character by doing another reading using the court card as the significator.

An Alternative Method

First, the querent should shuffle the entire pack and turn some of the cards round so that they are in the reversed position. The querent should then cut the pack with his or her left hand.

The querent should then deal out the first forty-two cards into six piles, each containing seven cards. The cards should be facing upwards, and the first seven cards dealt should form the first pile, the next set of seven cards should form the second pile, and so on until all forty-two cards are dealt. The end result should be like that in the diagram below.

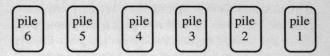

The querent should then pick up the first pile of cards and lay the cards in a row from right to left, as below:

The querent should then pick up the second pile of cards and place the cards on top of the cards of the first pile in the same order as before.

The querent should repeat this process until all the piles have been dealt out and seven new piles exist, as below:

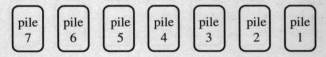

The querent should then take the top card of each new pile and shuffle them, then lay them out from right to left making a line of seven cards.

The querent should then take the next two cards from each pile and shuffle them together before laying them out in two lines of seven cards under the existing line.

Next the querent should pick up the remaining twenty-one cards and shuffle them before laying them out in three lines of seven cards below the existing three lines. The result should be that the querent has six lines of seven cards arranged in horizontal lines, as below:

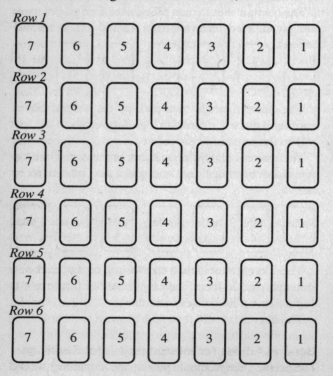

Row 1

| 7 | 6 | 5 | 4 | 3 | 2 | 1 |

Row 2

| 7 | 6 | 5 | 4 | 3 | 2 | 1 |

Row 3

| 7 | 6 | 5 | 4 | 3 | 2 | 1 |

Row 4

| 7 | 6 | 5 | 4 | 3 | 2 | 1 |

Row 5

| 7 | 6 | 5 | 4 | 3 | 2 | 1 |

Row 6

| 7 | 6 | 5 | 4 | 3 | 2 | 1 |

In this method the querent is represented by the Magician if the querent is male and by the High Priestess if the querent is female. The significator card should not be taken from the pack until after the forty-two cards have been laid out. If the Magician or High Priestess card is not among the cards laid out in the spread it will be found in the remaining thirty-six cards and should be placed a little to the right of the first horizontal line. If, however, the card is found among the forty-two cards it should be removed and placed as before. In this case another card should be randomly selected from the remaining thirty-six cards to fill the space.

The querent should then read the cards in succession from right to left, beginning at card number 1 of the top line at the extreme right. Therefore, the last card to be read will be the card at the extreme bottom left.

This spread is the most suitable when the querent does not wish to ask a specific question but does want some general guidance regarding his or her life and destiny. The querent can give general outlines such as the period of time he or she wishes to know about. However, these specifications should be made at the beginning of the process and concentrated on for the duration.

General Advice for Interpreting Tarot Readings
The person interpreting the cards (the divinator) should

remember that the interpretation of the cards must be made relevant to the querent and the question asked. The official and conventional meanings of the cards should be adapted to harmonise with the particular case in question – the position, time of life, and sex of the querent. The general trend of the cards should also be taken into consideration, and the divinator should allow intuition to play its role.

At the beginning of the reading the divinator should briefly run through the cards laid out to get a general impression of the subject – the trend of the destiny – and then read each card in detail.

The divinator should try to refrain from letting personal opinions interfere in the reading of the cards as this will alter the interpretation. It is obviously difficult to do this if one person is both the querent and the divinator, but it is important if a true reading is to be gained.

The Major Arcana

The Fool

Pictorial Symbolism

The picture shows the figure of a young man dressed in
fine, fancy clothes. He is paused at a precipice among

the heights of the world. His gaze is cast upon the skies above him rather than the drop below him. Although the figure is stationary, it is obvious by his stance and the dog's bounding that he has no intention of stopping. He shows no fear of the depths below him. It is as if he believes that if he should fall he will be caught and saved by angels. He appears to be in a dreamlike state. He carries a rose and an expensive wand that has an embroidered purse attached to it. He is the prince of the spiritual world on a journey through the world on a beautiful morning, bathed in sunlight.

Divinatory Meaning

The Fool card is 0 and is considered to represent the beginning of a spiritual journey. There is a focus on trust and hope, but this could be blind and reflects uncertainty on the part of the querent. It is a curious card as it highlights the uncertainties of life. Sometimes it is necessary to take an apparently risky step to make good. However, at other times it is wiser to stay put. This card's presence in a reading indicates to the querent that it is important to trust his or her judgment and plan for the future but to do so wisely. This is not a good time to make binding commitments. The Fool card represents trust, ideals, hope of a bright tomorrow, choice and folly.

Reversed Meaning

When the Fool card appears in the reversed position in a reading it represents negligence, absence, carelessness, apathy and vanity. The querent may be feeling eccentric at this time and be inclined to extravagant behaviour, but this could lead to his or her downfall.

Special Consideration

The Fool card is very much open to interpretation by the querent. The other cards in the reading may well give the querent more clarity.

The Magician

THE MAGICIAN.

Pictorial symbolism

The picture on the card depicts a representation of the energies of the universe. Above the magician's head is a

figure of eight on its side, which symbolises infinity and
the closed circle of energy. The serpent encircled round
the figure's waist and devouring its own tail symbolises
eternity.

Divinatory Meaning

The presence of a Major Arcana card will dominate a
reading and will carry more weight than Minor Arcana
cards. The Magician card is number one, and ones in
a reading indicate a new beginning and change. There
is a focus is on new beginnings and acting to realise
one's desires. The Magician card represents skill, di-
plomacy, subtlety, self-confidence and will. These are
all traits that the querent needs to draw on in order to
be able to achieve his or her goals. However, the
querent should exercise some caution as the Magician card can also represent treachery. The querent
may feel manipulated and exploited by another. In
this situation the querent should meditate and follow
his or her instincts.

Reversed Meaning

When the Magician card appears in the reversed position in a reading it represents disgrace, self-deceit, lies
and misuse of power. The querent may be involved in a
tricky situation and either the querent or another is lying in order to shift the blame.

Special Consideration

When the Magician card appears in a reading the querent must pay extra attention to the surrounding cards as they hold the key to what is beginning and why. The querent must then follow intuition in order to find the best course of action.

The High Priestess

THE HIGH PRIESTESS

Pictorial Symbolism

The figure in the picture represents a woman, as the High
Priestess card symbolises the feminine force. The card

represents mystery and magic, which is shown by the presence of the scroll inscribed with 'Tora', signifying the greater law and the second sense of the world. The crescent moon at the figure's feet symbolises the energies of the earth. She is seated between two pillars, one dark and one light, which indicate balance.

Divinatory Meaning

The presence of a Major Arcana card will dominate a reading and will carry more weight than Minor Arcana cards. The High Priestess card is number two, and twos in a reading indicate a period of gestation, of waiting and anticipation of great success in the future. There is a focus on waiting, gathering knowledge, and balance. The High Priestess card represents wisdom, mystery, understanding, gathering strength, intuition and serenity. The High Priestess card indicates a time of gestation before goals can be realised but also indicates the importance of using this time wisely to acknowledge inner changes and wait until one's energies are released. During this time of waiting the querent will quietly be gathering strength and knowledge that will prove useful in the future.

Reversed Meaning

When the High Priestess card appears in the reversed position in a reading it represents ignorance, conceit, surface knowledge and an immoral nature.

Special Consideration

The presence of this card indicates that the querent is troubled by the future and that this is causing problems. The High Priestess card symbolises truth and indicates that the future will be positive as the querent has new strengths to draw on.

The Empress

Pictorial Symbolism

The Empress card represents earthly paradise and shows a Venus-like figure in a field of corn with a waterfall

behind her. The Venus symbol in the picture shows that she is a representation of womanhood and motherhood. The twelve star cluster shows that her role is a universal one as these represent the twelve constellations of the zodiac.

Divinatory Meaning

The presence of a Major Arcana card will dominate a reading and will carry more weight than Minor Arcana cards. The Empress card is a number three, and threes in a reading suggest the involvement of more than more than one person and can also indicate that there will be a period of suspended activity before future successes. There is a focus on being rather than doing, on being in tune with one's inner feelings and emotions. The Empress card represents fruitfulness, feelings, emotions, development, creativity and fertility. The Empress card indicates that the querent will be rewarded as a result of fruitful labour. The querent should not be disillusioned by delays but trust his or her instincts and there will be success in the future.

Reversed Meaning

When the Empress card appears in the reversed position in a reading it represents idleness, ignorance, inaction and waste. The querent may feel uncertain at this time and may experience difficulties in expressing himself or herself. This will not last and is only a temporary state.

Special Consideration

The Empress card is a card that represents the emotions and indicates to the querent the importance of following instincts and feelings. The querent should not be redirected by thought and action.

The Emperor

THE EMPEROR.

Pictorial Symbolism

The Emperor card represents a powerful figure seated on a throne. He is clothed in a manner that shows his power. The staff that he holds in his right hand represents a wand, indicating his power in the spiritual world. The corners of his throne are fronted by two rams' heads, indicating an association with the astrological sign of Aries.

Divinatory Meaning

The presence of a Major Arcana card will dominate a reading and will carry more weight than Minor Arcana cards. The Emperor card is number four and fours in a reading indicate the realisation of one's goals. There is a focus on definite changes that will be obvious in the querent's life. The Emperor card represents strength, dominance, stability, power, authority, will, conviction and protection. The emperor card indicates that this is a time when new opportunities will present themselves to the querent, and if these opportunities have solid foundations they should bring the querent success. The querent should act promptly, without delay, but should allow for changes and be willing to make adaptations accordingly.

Reversed Meaning

When the Emperor card appears in the reversed position in a reading it represents immaturity, impulsiveness, obstruction and hastiness. The querent may be wasting a great deal of energy at this time by acting without thought and causing arguments.

Special Consideration

There is little spiritual guidance to be interpreted from the Emperor card as it is a very practical card with its roots in this world.

The Hierophant

Pictorial Symbolism

The Hierophant is seated on a throne – a different throne
from that on which the Emperor sits. The Hierophant's

throne indicates his power over the spiritual world. There are religious connections represented in this picture. The Hierophant holds a triple-cross sceptre in his left hand. The seven rounded points of the sceptre are associated with the seven deadly sins of Christianity. The Hierophant is frequently regarded as representing the pope or the head of the church. At the Hierophant's feet two figures are kneeling, showing respect and servitude to their teacher.

Divinatory Meaning

The presence of a Major Arcana card will dominate a reading and will carry more weight than Minor Arcana cards. The Hierophant card is number five, and fives in a reading indicate a time of changes and a period of ups and downs. There is a focus on the querent's relationships with others, groups and individuals. The querent is striving to find the truth and make sense of the changes in his or her life. The Hierophant card represents conventionality, captivity, servitude, marriage and alliance. This card shows the querent the importance of commitments to others and the strength of relationships. If the querent has concerns about a relationship, the presence of this card indicates that he or she should persevere and continue to work on the relationship.

Reversed Meaning

When the Hierophant card appears in the reversed position in a reading it represents weakness, gullibility, the need for tolerance and understanding. The querent may be involved with an individual whose behaviour is irritating and self-indulgent. However annoying this person is, the best course of action is for the querent to show tolerance.

Special Consideration
The querent should be inspired to achieve greater spiritual understanding by clearing his or her mind of feelings and thoughts that belong in the past.

The Lovers

Pictorial Symbolism

The picture shows two figures – one male and one female. Their nudity suggests youth, innocence, love and

purity. Comparisons can be made to Adam and Eve. The winged figure in the background represents Cupid. The trees behind the figures are the Tree of Life and the Tree of Knowledge. This card is simply a representation of human love.

Divinatory Meaning

The presence of a Major Arcana card will dominate a reading and will carry more weight than Minor Arcana cards. The Lovers card is number six, and sixes in a reading indicate adaptability and the ability to change in times of difficulty. There is a focus on love, relationships and change. The Lovers card represents attraction, love, beauty, romance, harmony and trials overcome. This card indicates to the querent that a new relationship will be successful and of deeper significance than previously experienced. If the querent is already involved in a relationship, this card shows that any problems will be overcome and that old bonds are still strong. The querent should be wary of taking things at surface value and should be aware that situations that appear to be negative may well come good in time.

Reversed Meaning

When the Lovers card appears in the reversed position in a reading it represents failure, the break-up of a relationship, frustration and division. The querent may experience difficulties in a relationship, which will result in insecurity. However, the relationship may be salvaged providing that both parties wish it to be so.

Special Consideration
This card is very much concerned with fate and divine power. It shows that the querent should keep faith in order to prosper.

The Chariot

Pictorial Symbolism

The figure shown in the picture symbolises control and conquest on all planes. Although he is a princely figure, he is not a member of a priesthood. Therefore the conquests that he has made are manifest or external and not within himself. He does not hold the answer to spiritual questions.

Divinatory Meaning

The presence of a Major Arcana card will dominate a reading and will carry more weight than Minor Arcana cards. The Chariot card is number seven, and sevens in a reading indicate a time of solitude and of questioning oneself. There is a focus on identifying problems by asking oneself searching questions while heeding the importance of learning lessons from previous mistakes. The Chariot card represents change, providence, triumph, problems overcome and troubles. The key to the Chariot card is to take control of a situation while remembering the importance of compromise. Once the querent has identified the cause of the problem, all aspects of his or her life will begin to progress and improve.

Reversed Meaning

When the Chariot card appears in the reversed position in a reading it represents litigation, dispute, defeat, quarrelling and failure. The querent may find at this time that it is easy to become involved in arguments over petty matters. One such argument could lead to litigation, which would result in the querent being defeated.

Special Consideration
The Chariot card represent the storm before the calm. It is a powerful card that promotes immediate action. The querent should be alert and try to remain in control in order to succeed.

Strength

Pictorial Symbolism

The picture shows a young woman closing the jaws of a lion, demonstrating her power over nature. It can be seen that the lion is already calmed and tamed by the nature of the woman as she is leading it by a chain of flowers. The lion signifies passions, and she who is called Strength is the higher nature in its liberation.

Divinatory Meaning

The presence of a Major Arcana card will dominate a reading and will carry more weight than Minor Arcana cards. The Strength card is number eight, and eights in a reading are very positive and indicate positive changes. There is a focus on fortitude and courage. The querent should be true to convictions and challenge those who are in the wrong. The querent will need to have courage and determination in order to succeed. Success will result in the querent being respected as a leader and a source of inspiration. The Strength card represents power, energy, action, courage, success and balance. This is a very positive card, which should motivate the querent to have faith in himself or herself.

Reversed Meaning

When the Strength card appears in the reversed position in a reading it represents weakness, discord, disgrace and lack of faith. The presence of this card suggests that disharmony has resulted from the abuse of power, leaving others resentful and bitter.

Special Meaning

The Strength card in a reading should inspire the querent to face up to situations that may appear to be difficult. This will develop the querent's confidence and self-esteem and help him or her to retain his or her sense of purpose.

The Hermit

THE HERMIT.

Pictorial Symbolism

The figure in the picture is dressed in ancient robes and carries a lantern containing a shining star. This represents the blending of the idea of the Ancient of Days with the Light of the World. The beacon that the figure holds intimates 'where I am, you may also be'.

Divinatory Meaning

The presence of a Major Arcana card will dominate a reading and will carry more weight than Minor Arcana cards. The Hermit card is number nine, and nines in a reading indicate the completion of events. There is a focus on an important situation in the querent's life. The querent may well be about to progress on to a new stage of life but needs to remove any difficulties from the current situation in order to be able to make the progression. The querent may have recently experienced difficulties that resulted in loneliness and isolation. Once the querent feels that this situation is entirely in the past, he or she will be able to help others experiencing similar difficulties. The Hermit card represents wisdom, prudence, solitude, faith and discrimination. This card indicates that the querent is self-aware and this self-knowing will prove useful in achieving greater wisdom and understanding.

Reversed Meaning

When the Hermit card appears in the reversed position in a reading it represents a lack of faith, unreasoned caution, concealment and a closed heart and mind. The querent may be feeling a desire to be detached from those close to him or her, but the motivation is wrong and the action is cold-hearted.

Special Consideration

The Hermit card indicates to the querent the need to face up to imperfections. It is necessary to come to terms with and accept these in order to allow development. The querent should strive to divest himself or herself of thoughts of distrust and reservation.

The Wheel of Fortune

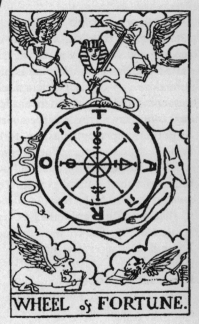

Pictorial Symbolism
The wheel depicted on the card symbolises the flux of human life and the perpetual motion of the universe.

The Sphinx symbolises the equilibrium and stability amid movement.

Divinatory Meaning

The presence of a Major Arcana card will dominate a reading and will carry more weight than Minor Arcana cards. The Wheel of Fortune is number ten and therefore a one ($1 + 0 = 1$). Ones in a reading indicate a new beginning and change. There is a focus on potential success following changes in the querent's life. The Wheel of Fortune represents destiny, fortune, success, elevation, luck and change. The presence of this card in a reading indicates to the querent that it is important to let things run their natural course. The querent would be well advised to make few plans as these may well have to changed. This card indicates that the key to success is adaptability. The changes that occur in the querent's life will be of a positive nature.

Reversed Meaning

When the Wheel of Fortune appears in the reversed position in a reading it represents bad luck, uncertainty and decline. The querent may find that changes occurring in one area of his or her life have a negative effect on another area. In order to identify which area may suffer, the querent should pay close attention to the other cards in the reading as they will hold the answer.

Special Consideration

Out of chaos a new start will emerge for the querent.
The other cards in the reading are especially obtaining
an exact interpretation of the significance of the Wheel
of Fortune. The other cards will determine the direction
and influence of the change.

Justice

Pictorial Symbolism

The figure in the picture is seated between two pillars – in a similar position to that of the High Priestess. The pillars of justice open on one world and the pillars of the High Priestess onto another. In this instance the pillars open onto the world of spiritual and moral justice. The card of Justice symbolises the scales, and the sword indicates a balance of mercy and retribution.

Divinatory Meaning

The presence of a Major Arcana card will dominate a reading and will carry more weight than Minor Arcana cards. The Justice card is number eleven and therefore a two (1 + 1 = 2). Twos in a reading indicate a period of gestation, of waiting and anticipation of future success. There is a focus on matters concerning the law or partnerships. The Justice card represents equality, rightness, triumph and balance. The presence of the Justice card indicates to the querent that if he or she is involved in a legal dispute the hearing will be just and fair, and the outcome will probably favour the querent.

Reversed Meaning

When the Justice card appears in the reversed position in a reading it represents legal complications, bigotry, bias and excessive severity. The querent's behaviour may have been excessive of late, and this may result in repercussions, perhaps in the form of a fine.

Special Consideration

The Justice card indicates to the querent the importance
of achieving a balance within oneself as well as in one's
surroundings. This cannot be rushed, however, and time
must be allowed to run its course.

The Hanged Man

THE HANGED MAN.

Pictorial Symbolism

The figure is suspended from a cross while his body
also forms a cross. The Hanged Man is a curious card

because of the contradictions that are apparent. Despite the fact that the man is hanging by his neck, his face expresses deep entrancement. He has a nimbus round his head. The figure is hanging from wood that is obviously living as it is covered with leaves. This card symbolises life in suspension rather than death, which may appear to be the first impression.

Divinatory Meaning

The presence of a Major Arcana card will dominate a reading and will carry more weight than Minor Arcana cards. The Hanged Man card is number twelve and therefore a three $(1 + 2 = 3)$. Threes in a reading indicate a period of suspended activity before future success can be achieved. There is a focus on reflecting on what is happening here and now. The querent should think of ways in which he or she can make compromises in order to avoid failure. The Hanged Man represents wisdom, circumspection, discernment, trials, sacrifice, intuition, divination, prophecy and change. This card reveals that the querent is experiencing an awakening of his or her intuitive powers, and he or she will find this enriches his or her life.

Reversed Meaning

When the Hanged Man appears in the reversed position in a reading it represents selfishness, the crowd, lack of effort and lack of compromise. The querent may find it difficult to progress at this time as he or she is acting stubbornly and making no compromises. This behaviour could well result in the querent experiencing losses, perhaps losing friends.

Special Consideration

The Hanged Man serves as a reminder to the querent of the importance of intuition and psychic powers that defy scientific explanation.

Death

Pictorial Symbolism

Death is represented by one of the apocalyptic visions.
Behind the figure of Death lies the whole world of as-

cent in the spirit. The mysterious horseman moves slowly, bearing a black banner emblazoned with the mystic rose that signifies life. Between two pillars on the verge of the horizon the sun of immortality shines. The horseman carries no visible weapon but falling in front of him are a king, a child and a maiden, and a man of the church awaits his end with clasped hands.

Divinatory Meaning

The presence of a Major Arcana card will dominate a reading and will carry more weight than Minor Arcana cards. The Death card is number thirteen and therefore a four (1 + 3 = 4). Fours in a reading indicate the realisation of one's goals. There is a focus on endings and beginnings, good and bad. The Death card represents changes, endings, morality, corruption, rebirth and beginnings. The presence of the Death card indicates to the querent that a stage in his or her life is coming to an end but that from this ending new experiences will evolve. Once the ending is complete the querent will be able to progress to the future and let go of the past.

Reversed Meaning

When the Death card appears in the reversed position in a reading it represents stagnation, inertia, lethargy and destruction. The querent may lack motivation at this time and be constantly looking for courses of action that require little effort. The querent should try to find enthusiasm for life or the destructive nature of this behaviour will take its toll.

Special Consideration

The Death card indicates to the querent that it is necessary to look at what is happening in his or her life and to question the amount of energy that he or she is putting into relationships that are not progressing. The querent needs to decide whether it is necessary to let go in order to save energy.

Temperance

Pictorial Symbolism

In the picture there is a figure of a winged angel with the sign of the sun on its forehead. On its breast it has the square and triangle of the septenary (the number seven). The figure is pouring the essences of life from one chalice to another. The angel stands with one foot on the earth and with one foot in the water, which illustrates the nature of the essences of life. To the left of the figure there is a path leading to a range of mountains on the distant horizon. Above the mountain range is a great light – part of the secret of eternal life lies here.

Divinatory Meaning

The presence of a Major Arcana card will dominate a reading and will carry more weight than Minor Arcana cards. The Temperance card is the number fourteen and therefore a five (1 + 4 = 5). Fives in a reading indicate a time of changes and of ups and downs. There is a focus on reassessing situations that seemed to be behind the querent but have re-emerged. The Temperance card represents moderation, frugality, management, accommodation and economy. The presence of the Temperance card in a reading indicates to the querent that it is necessary to live frugally and manage affairs carefully at this time.

Reversed Meaning

When the Temperance card is in the reversed position in a reading it represents conflicts, competing interests, divisions and hostilities. The querent may be feeling self-indulgent at this time, which could lead to those involved with the querent being angered by his or her selfish behaviour. The result of this situation could well be disputes and arguments. To avoid this the querent should act less selfishly and be more considerate of others.

Special Consideration

The Temperance card indicates to the querent that he or she is entering into a time of recuperation, both spiritually and physically. At this time it is important to keep distractions to a minimum in order to allow the process of healing to be completed.

The Devil

Pictorial Symbolism

The card shows a figure, the Horned Goat of Mendes, with wings like those of a bat, standing on an altar. At the pit of his stomach there is the sign of Mercury. The right hand is upraised and extended, being the reverse of the benediction given by the Hierophant. In the figure's left hand there is a great flaming torch inverted towards the earth. A reversed pentagram is on the forehead. There is a ring in front of the altar from which two chains are carried to the necks of two figures, one male and one female. These are analogous with those on the fifth card, as if Adam and Eve after their fall from grace.

Divinatory Meaning

The presence of a Major Arcana card will dominate a reading and will carry more weight than Minor Arcana cards. The Devil card is number fifteen, therefore a six (1 + 5 = 6). When there are sixes in a reading it indicates adaptability and the need to make changes in times of difficulty. This card usually indicates that the querent is involved in a negative situation but that his or her ability to get out of it is low due to clouded judgment. It represents violence, force, failure, disaster, death and ominous events. When the querent draws the Devil card it signifies that the querent should reflect on the present situation and ask others for advice. The querent should work towards solving difficulties cautiously and slowly.

Reversed Meaning

When the Devil card appears in the reversed position in

a reading it represents weakness, pettiness and blindness. The querent may be experiencing a weakness of the spirit at this time and therefore be blind to faults, both his or her own and others. Such blindness and lack of perception may cause the querent harm, and he or she should try to find strength at this time.

Special Consideration

Although the Devil card has a sinister quality, it should not be feared. This card indicates to the querent that it is necessary to focus energies on positive thoughts and actions instead of draining oneself by wasting energy on negative aspects.

The Tower

Pictorial Symbolism

On the surface this card depicts ruin in all its aspects.
The Tower is said to be derived from the Tower of Babel,

which is written about in the Bible as well as other historical works. One version of events tells how the Tower of Babel contained all the knowledge of the world in a library. God destroyed this library to show that knowledge alone does not make a person great; a person needs humility and wisdom in order to make sense and good use of knowledge. This interpretation of the Tower then indicates that the Tower is symbolic of false hopes and ideas.

Divinatory Meaning

The presence of a Major Arcana card will dominate a reading and will carry more weight than Minor Arcana cards. The Tower card is a number seven card (1 + 6 = 7). When readings contain sevens, it indicates a time of solitude and asking questions of oneself. When the Tower card is drawn in a reading there is a focus on sudden and complete change, unexpected events and separations. When the querent draws the Tower card it is nearly always an indication of unwelcome change. The Tower card represents misery, distress, adversity, deception and ruin. The querent would be well advised to seek advice and help. It is important for the querent not to lose heart as it is possible to rebuild after changes. The other cards in the reading will indicate which area of the querent's life is subject to change and to what extent the querent will suffer.

Reversed Meaning

When the Tower card is drawn in the reversed position in a reading it represents oppression, imprisonment, tyranny and ongoing depression. The querent may feel dominated by another or by a situation and will feel powerless to fight back at this time. The querent should concentrate on the future and on ways to redress the balance of power.

Special Meaning

The Tower card should be seen as an indication that the time has come to make a new start. The querent should have inner peace and be aware of the whole picture rather than be held back by dwelling on the negative changes.

The Star

Pictorial Symbolism

The main feature on the card is a large radiant with eight rams surrounded by seven similar but smaller stars. In the foreground there is a figure of a naked woman. She has her left knee on the land while her right foot rests on the water. She has in her hand two vases from which she pours Water of Life – one into the sea and one onto the land. Behind the figure there is a bird resting in a shrub on a hill. The figure represents eternal youth and beauty. The Star card represents hope and the beauty of the natural world.

Divinatory Meaning

The presence of a Major Arcana card will dominate a reading and will carry more weight than Minor Arcana cards. The Star card is a number eight card $(1 + 7 = 8)$, and eights in a reading are very positive and indicate positive changes. When the Star card is drawn in a reading, there is a focus on what may lie ahead in the future. The Star card indicates to the querent that recent difficulties will soon disappear and a new more positive future will begin. The Star card represents hope, bright prospects, new opportunities and just rewards. On drawing this card, the querent should feel a sense of relief and calm. The querent may well experience new independence and inner strength in the near future.

Reversed Meaning

When the Star card appears in the reversed position in a reading it represents loss, impotence and lack of success. The querent may experience temporary setbacks and may be easily taken in by a conman or be the victim of a theft.

Special Consideration
The Star shines a light of hope and promise on the querent. It is sometimes said that the Star card rewards a faith in oneself and in fate.

The Moon

THE MOON .

Pictorial Symbolism

In the centre of the picture there is the moon with sixteen main and sixteen secondary rays. From the fore-

ground of the picture, winding its way up to the hills, is a path leading to the unknown. Also in the foreground there is a dog and a wolf, representing the fears of the natural mind in the presence of the unknown. The presence of the dog, wolf and a creature from the sea have been interpreted as illuminations of our animal nature, with the sea creature representing the part of our nature that is lower than a savage beast. In the picture the creature is trying to attain manifestation by crawling out of the water. But as a rule it will generally sink back. The moon directs a calm face on the unrest below.

Divinatory Meaning

The presence of a Major Arcana card will dominate a reading and will carry more weight than Minor Arcana cards. The Moon card is number eighteen and therefore a nine card (1 + 8 = 9). Nines in a reading indicate the completion of events. When the Moon card is drawn in a reading there is a focus on inner fears and uncertainties. The Moon card indicates that the querent would be wise to pay attention to intuitive feelings and inner voices. The querent should be wary, as at this time he or she is open to threats and dangers. The Moon card represents hidden enemies, danger, darkness, deception and errors.

Reversed Meaning

When the Moon card appears in the reversed position in

a reading, it represents instability, inconsistency, silence and minor problems. The querent may be involved in a difficult situation at this time, which is adversely affecting his or her health and inner strength.

Special Consideration
The Moon card shows the querent that at some point it will be necessary for him or her to face up to the situation and accept it for what it is in order to make any changes. The Moon card should inspire the querent to be true to himself or herself.

The Sun

Pictorial Symbolism

In the foreground there is the figure of a naked child mounted on a white horse. The child represents simplicity and innocence in humanity. Behind the figure is a walled garden spilling forth life in all forms. The sun dominates the horizon, being the source of light and warmth for the earth below. Without the sun there would be no life on earth. The child figure is outside the walled garden and is making the transition from the known world of earth into the unknown world beyond.

Divinatory Meaning

The presence of a Major Arcana card will dominate a reading and will carry more weight than Minor Arcana cards. The Sun card is number nineteen and therefore a one card (1 + 9 = 10 and 1 + 0 = 1). Ones in a reading indicate new beginnings and change. When the Sun card is drawn in a reading, there is a focus on relationships with others and on self-knowledge. The Sun card indicates that the querent is contented with his or her position in life and knows inner peace and that success and happiness will be ongoing. This is very positive card. The Sun card represents material happiness, contentment, accomplishment and successful unions. If the querent is contemplating marriage or commitment, this card indicates that it will be a successful union.

Reversed Meaning

When the Sun card appears in the reversed position in a reading it represents minor successes but the querent should be wary of over committing himself or herself and should exercise caution. The querent may feel pompous and vain at this time, which could result in a blurring of judgment and the querent may be persuaded to make rash decisions.

Special Consideration
The presence of this card in a reading indicates a very positive stage in the querent's life. The querent has achieved a new level of spiritual maturity and is now benefiting from this.

Judgement

Pictorial Symbolism

There is a figure of a great angel encompassed by clouds.
The angel blows a trumpet that has a banner bearing a

cross attached to it. Below the angel, the dead are rising from their tombs. All the risen figures show wonder, adoration and ecstasy. The scene shows the awakening of awareness and spiritual enlightenment that are not possible to achieve in this life. It is a representation of eternal life.

Divinatory Meaning

The presence of a Major Arcana card will dominate a reading and will carry more weight than Minor Arcana cards. The Judgement card is number twenty and therefore a number two card (2 + 0 = 2). Twos in a reading indicate a period of gestation, of warmth and anticipation of future successes. When the Judgement card is drawn in a reading, there is a focus on change and new developments. The Judgement card indicates to the querent that it is important to deal with matters that have been previously put aside in order to advance to new successes. The Judgement card often indicates that there will be significant changes in the querent's life – new relationships, a new career or a new home. The Judgement card represents change of position, renewal and spiritual development.

Reversed Meaning

When the Judgement card appears in the reversed position in a reading it represents weakness, delays, deliberation, indecision and regrets. The querent may be involved in a legal dispute, and the presence of this card suggests that the decision will go against the querent, and the querent may regret his or her previous behaviour.

Special Consideration

The Judgement card will highlight any injustices that exist in the querent's life. The querent should be inspired to work towards the future and accept that there may not be any signs of material success for a while.

The World

Pictorial Symbolism

The World card represents the completed journey of the
Fool. The Fool has found freedom and the struggles of

life have been temporarily suspended. The figure on the card holds two wands, symbolising power on earth. These figures show the development of man. The figure has the attention of the four elements of the world – earth, fire, water and air – represented by the four figures outside her oval.

Divinatory Meaning

The presence of a Major Arcana card will dominate a reading and will carry more weight than Minor Arcana cards. The World is number twenty-one and therefore a three card (2 + 1 = 3). Threes in a reading suggest that there is more than one person involved and can also indicate that there will be a period of suspended activity before future success. When the World card is drawn in a reading, there is a focus on a significant change in the querent's life. This card could indicate that the querent may move overseas for a period. It shows that the querent has completed his or her inner journey and is now knowing inner peace at this stage in life. The World card indicates assured success, voyage, emigration and goals achieved.

Reversed Meaning

When the World card appears in the reversed position in a reading it represents inertia, stagnation and permanence. The querent may lack courage and conviction at this time. An opportunity may arise and the querent will have to act quickly and decisively. If he or she does not take advantage of this opportunity there may be regrets in the future.

Special Consideration
The querent should regard the presence of the World card as an inspiration to seize the day and attempt to fulfil his or her desires. If the querent is contemplating a significant change this card indicates that it will be successful.

The Minor Arcana

Ace of Wands

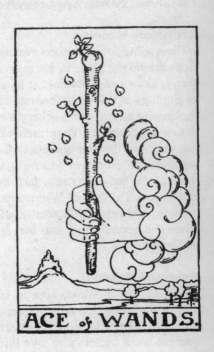

Pictorial Symbolism

In the picture there is a hand clasping a stout wand. The hand is emerging from a cloud and the wand is sprouting new leaves. The new leaves indicate that this is a card connected with new beginnings and life.

Divinatory Meaning

If the reading contains many Wands, it signifies that notions are taking place in the querent's mind. When an Ace is drawn in a reading, it is an indication of new beginnings as it is a number one card. The focus is on the querent achieving his or her potential and being open to new opportunities. The presence of this card in a reading indicates that the querent is feeling energised and ambitious. The querent will be inclined to make ambitious plans, but others may lack the same enthusiasm and vision. The Ace of Wands represents creation, invention, enterprise, birth, family, origin, virility and fortune. The querent may also feel spiritually awakened and enlightened.

Reversed Meaning

When the Ace of Wands appears in the reversed position in a reading it represents decadence, ruin, perdition, false start and blind optimism. It shows that the querent has a tendency to take things to the extreme. The querent may cause offence to others by being rude and tactless, the result of which could be disastrous for the querent.

Special Consideration

The Ace of Wands is a very powerful card that signifies awakening energies. The querent should be conscious of all new opportunities even from unsuspected sources. Keeping an open mind is very important.

Two of Wands

Pictorial Symbolism

In the centre of the picture there is a tall man dressed in robes. He is looking out over a battlement to the sea and shore in the distance. In his right hand he holds a globe. His left hand holds a wand that is resting on the battlement. The other wand is standing to the figure's right, secured by a metal ring. The figure is thought to be a lord surveying his domain but wistfully comparing his grandeur to the globe.

Divinatory Meaning

Twos in a reading indicate a period of gestation, of waiting and anticipation, and of great success in the future. If the reading contains many Wands, it signifies that notions are taking shape in the querent's mind. When the Two of Wands is drawn there is a focus on the querent's relationship to others. This card indicates a need for independence and solitude. The Two of Wands represents boldness, restricted freedom, dominance from another and separation. The querent may feel the need for a separation in order to feel in control of his or her destiny.

Reversed Meaning

When the Two of Wands appears in the reversed position it represents sadness, trouble, fear and loss. Although the querent may feel low at this point, change is imminent and hope should not be lost.

Special Consideration

The querent should assert his or her independence and

not allow others to deny him or her this freedom. He or she should not allow him or her to be drawn into something against his or her will. Be strong or you may have regrets.

Three of Wands

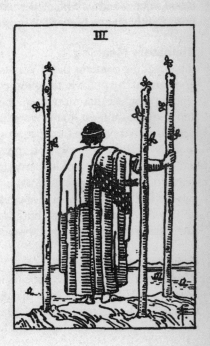

Pictorial Symbolism

In the centre of the picture is a stately figure with his back
turned. He is standing on the edge of a cliff and looking

out to sea. On the sea there are ships sailing. Around the figure three wands are planted in the ground. The figure leans lightly on one of the wands, gaining support.

Divinatory Meaning

If the reading contains many Wands, it signifies that notions are taking place in the querent's mind. Threes in a reading suggest that more than one person is involved and can also suggest that there will be a period of suspended activity before future successes are realised. The focus is on cooperation and business opportunities. This indicates a time of moving forward and activity. The Three of Wands represents established strength, enterprise, effort, trade, commerce and discovery. The querent will feel pleased with how things are going but should remember those who helped to make it possible.

Reversed Meaning

When the Three of Wands appears in the reversed position in a reading it represents disappointments, toil and treachery. The querent will find others to be uncooperative and should be wary of mixed loyalties.

Special Consideration

The querent should be optimistic but should concentrate only on aspirations and goals that can be realised in order to avoid disappointments.

Four of Wands

Pictorial Symbolism

In the foreground of the picture there are four wands planted in the ground. A great garland is suspended from the wands. In the centre there are two female figures holding bunches of flowers above their heads. They stand beside a bridge, over a moat, which leads to an old manor house.

Divinatory Meaning

If the reading contains many Wands, it signifies that notions are taking place in the querent's mind. Fours in a reading indicate the realisation of one's goals. There is a focus on relationships. This is a positive card that indicates that relationships are going well or that problems will soon pass. The Four of Wands represents harmony, haven, romance, peace, concord and prosperity. This card indicates to the querent a quiet time spent with friends and family in a favourite place.

Reversed Meaning

When the Four of Wands appears in the reversed position in a reading its meaning does not alter and is therefore equally positive.

Special Consideration

The querent should enjoy this period when he or she will experience inner peace as well as harmony with others. This card indicates that a very positive time will be enjoyed by the querent.

Five of Wands

Pictorial Symbolism

A group of youths can be seen to be brandishing wands. They are staging a conflict. There is a con-

nection to the battle of life, and the energies involved
therein.

Divinatory Meaning

If the reading contains many Wands, it signifies that
notions are taking place in the querent's mind. Fives
in a reading indicate a time of changes and of ups and
downs. There is a focus on inner conflicts and a clash
of personal ambitions. The presence of this card indicates the need for a struggle or confrontation in order
to move on from a situation that has become stagnant.
The Five of Wands represents strenuous competition,
gain and courage. The querent needs inner strength and
resolve in order to weather the storm, and this card in
a reading shows that he or she has the strength that is
required.

Reversed Meaning

When the Five of Wands appears in the reversed position
it represents litigation, disputes, trickery, complications,
contradictions and frustrations. The reversal of this card
indicates more negative and bitter struggles that may result in the unpleasant sides to people's characters appear-
ing.

Special consideration

It is important for the querent to be honest with himself

or herself about what he or she wants or needs. Once the querent establishes his or her desire, he or she is in a position to fight to win.

Six of Wands

Pictorial Symbolism

A Horseman wearing a laurel crown carries a wand also
bearing a laurel crown. At his side are footmen carrying

more wands. The scene indicates victory and trauma.

Divinatory Meaning

If the reading contains many Wands, it signifies that notions are taking place in the querent's mind. Sixes in a reading indicate adaptability and the ability to change in times of difficulty. There is a focus on success and victory. This card indicates deserved victory after a period of struggle. The querent could well receive some great news that will enhance the victory. The Six of Wands represents triumph, victory, good news, high expectations, glory, hope and advancement. The querent should take the time to celebrate. He or she has faced some difficult times previously and is now in a position to relax and be happy.

Reversed Meaning

When the Six of Wands appears in the reversed position it represents apprehension, fear, treachery, disloyalty and vulnerability. The querent feels uneasy and needs to face up to his or her adversaries in order to clear the air.

Special Consideration

The querent would be well advised to offer friendship and conciliation to old adversaries rather than gloat about his or her success. The querent will be far happier within himself or herself once efforts have been made to repair friendships.

Seven
of Wands

Pictorial Symbolism

A young man standing on the edge of a precipice brandishes a wand while six other wands point up towards

him from below. The figure's face shows strength and
determination in the face of what appears to be an enemy that outnumbers him.

Divinatory Meaning
If the reading contains many Wands, it signifies thought.
Sevens in a reading represent a time of solitude and asking questions of oneself. The focus is on courage. The
querent has already displayed courage by standing up to
a problem and ongoing strength will be needed in order
to continue with the fight. The Seven of Wands represents valour, discussion, difficult negotiations, competition in business, and success over enemies. The odds may
be against the querent but he or she should stand firm.

Reversed Meaning
When the Seven of Wands appears in the reversed position it represents embarrassments, anxiety and confusion. The querent should be warned against indecision
as it can lead to an adversary taking advantage.

Special Consideration
The querent should not only concentrate on challenges
externally but also within. In order to progress the
querent should be prepared to make changes to himself
or herself by challenging that which requires improve-
ment.

Eight of Wands

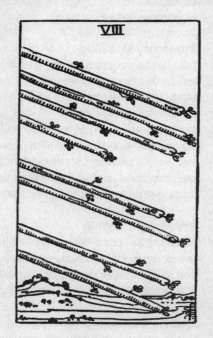

Pictorial Symbolism

Eight wands can be seen to be flying through open country, representing motion through the immovable. The

wands are drawing towards the term of their course –
they are on the threshold of that which they signify.

Divinatory Meaning

If the reading contains many Wands, it signifies that notions are taking place in the querent's mind. Eights in a
reading are very positive and represent positive changes.
There is a focus on fast-moving events and actions. If
the querent is waiting for a reply to a letter, he or she
will not have long to wait. The response could contain
the promise of new love. The Eight of Wands represents
swiftness, great haste, great hope, Cupid's arrow of love,
and assured felicity. If a situation has been stagnant for
some time, the querent may be surprised by a rapid progression towards a conclusion.

Reversed Meaning

When the Eight of Wands appears in the reversed position
in a reading it represents jealously, internal dispute, stingings
of conscience, quarrels, domestic disputes and lack of harmony. This situation could be brought about by an impetu-
ous letter of hasty and ill-thought-out comment.

Special Consideration

The querent is aware of his or her desires and should
take the initiative to realise them. This is a positive time
and a time to make changes.

Nine of Wands

Pictorial Symbolism

In the centre of the picture a figure leans on a wand. He has an expectant, suspicious look on his face, as if he is awaiting his enemies. Behind him stand eight more wands standing in an orderly row.

Divinatory Meaning

If the reading contains many Wands, it signifies that notions are taking place in the querent's mind. Nines in a reading indicate the completion of events. There is a focus on strength in opposition. It indicates that there could be a suspension of events, with the querent having the advantage at the present time. The presence of this card suggests that there has been conflict previously and there could be more ahead. The Nine of Wands represents boldness, readiness, strength, suspension, delay and adjournment. This card could signify that the querent is recovering from an illness.

Reversed Meaning

When the Nine of Wands appears in the reversed position it represents obstacles, adversity, calamity and a lack of initiative.

Special Consideration

The querent should not lose faith. He or she will need to be strong at this time in order to deal with future complications. The outlook in the long term is more positive.

Ten of Wands

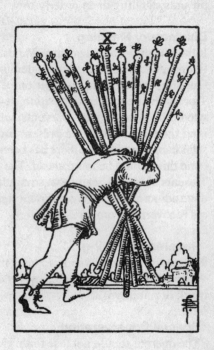

Pictorial Symbolism

The picture shows a figure struggling to carry ten wands to a distant place. He is succeeding in the task but obviously finds it a burden as his posture indicates oppression.

Divinatory Meaning

If the reading contains many Wands, it signifies that notions are taking place in the querent's mind. (1 + 0 = 1). Ones in a reading indicate new beginnings and change. The focus is on success but success that has little reward. The presence of this card indicates that the querent is not at peace with himself or herself and is acting in a selfish manner. The querent may well receive material rewards at this time but spiritually this is a poor time. The Ten of Wands represents material gain, oppression, disguise, selfishness and excessive demands. If the querent is involved in a lawsuit he or she will almost certainly face defeat.

Reversed Meaning

When the Ten of Wands appears in the reversed position in a reading it represents contrarieties, difficulties, intrigues and deceit. The querent should be aware of others conspiring against him or her unexpectedly.

Special Consideration

To regain inner peace the querent should try to be more generous to others, both emotionally and materially. Material success is far more rewarding if the gains are shared.

Page of Wands

PAGE of WANDS.

Pictorial Symbolism

The figure of a young man stands holding a wand. He stands as if about to deliver an important message.

Divinatory Meaning

If the reading contains many Wands, it signifies that notions are taking place in the querent's mind. The Page of Wands represents the astrological sign of Sagittarius. The focus is on receiving news. The querent should expect to receive good news that will cheer him or her. It could also indicate that a young man will be a faithful friend during a difficult time. The Page of Wands in a reading represents faithfulness, a postman, a lover, an envoy, a messenger, consistency and stability. This card can also indicate that family problems will come to an end.

Reversed Meaning

When the Page of Wands appears in the reversed position in a reading it represents bad news, indecision, instability and reluctance. A young person could be the source of bad news.

Special Consideration

A close friend could help to enlighten the querent, and the querent could see things from a new perspective.

Knight
of Wands

KNIGHT of WANDS.

Pictorial Symbolism

A figure in armour charges across the landscape. Despite his dress, however, his mission is not a warlike one.

Divinatory Meaning

If the reading contains many Wands, it signifies that notions are taking place in the querent's mind. The presence of a knight in a reading indicates that a situation will soon change. The focus is on the need to make important decisions. The querent could be making a journey abroad. Other changes that may be happening in the querent's life could be a new residence, a new relationship or a new business connection. The Knight of Wands represents departure, absence, flight, emigration and change of residence. The querent may find himself or herself receptive to prophetic visions at this time.

Reversed Meaning

When the Knight of Wands appears in the reversed position in a reading it represents rupture, division, interruption, discord and conflict. This state of affairs could be brought about by a person making offensive remarks.

Special Consideration

The realisation of the querent's goals is imminent and the querent should continue to have faith.

Queen of Wands

QUEEN of WANDS.

Pictorial Symbolism

The queen sits on her throne holding a wand in her right
hand and a sunflower in her left hand. At her feet sits a

black cat. The queen has a mystical appearance. She is a proud woman who has the ability to be both loving and tyrannical.

Divinatory Meaning

If the reading contains many Wands, it signifies that notions are taking place in the querent's mind. The Queen of Wands is associated with the astrological sign Leo. The focus is on family matters and relationships. This card indicates that the querent will encounter a friendly and loving woman. This woman may bring the querent success in business. The Queen of Wands represents a woman – friendly, chaste, loving, honourable – success in business and material gain.

Reversed Meaning

When the Queen of Wands appears in the reversed position in a reading it represents jealously, deceit, a turned friend, false pride, snobbery and stupidity.

Special Consideration

After a lull the querent's spiritual development will be renewed. It is important to seek advice from others during this time.

King of Wands

KING of WANDS

Pictorial Symbolism

The king sits on his throne holding a wand in his hand.
He is leaning forward on his throne in a manner that

suggests that he is both animated and ardent. Behind him, on the back of his throne, the symbol of the lion is emblazoned and this is an appropriate symbol to represent the King of Wands.

Divinatory Meaning

If the reading contains many Wands, it signifies that notions are taking place in the querent's mind. The King of Wands is linked with the astrological sign of Aries. The presence of this card in a reading indicates that there is a focus on the querent's ambitions. This card indicates that the querent will have a favourable encounter with an assertive male who will support the querent during a difficult time. As a result of this encounter the querent may benefit financially. The King of Wands in a reading represents honesty, unexpected inheritance, friendship, nobility and loyalty.

Reversed Meaning

When the King of Wands appears in the reversed position in a reading it represents unpredictability, bigotry, contradictory behaviour on another's part and severity. The querent should be wary of characters whose integrity is doubtful, and he or she should be prepared to remain calm in a possible crisis.

Special Consideration

Although the querent will gain much from the support of the male that he or she will meet, it is important to remember one's own strengths and abilities. This is a time during which the querent is feeling confident and should use this confidence to inspire others whose situations are less favourable.

Ace of Cups

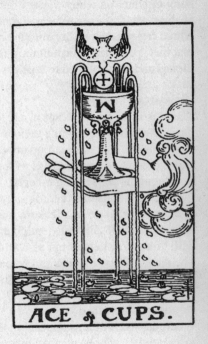

Pictorial Symbolism

In the centre of the picture is a cup held in the palm of a
hand. From the cup four streams are flowing and the hand

is emerging from a cloud. The hand is suspended above a body of water on which water lilies are floating. A dove bearing what appears to be a communion wafer marked with a cross is descending into the cup. All this indicates that this is a spiritual or religious card, which celebrates the mysticism attributed to chalices throughout time.

Divinatory Meaning

The presence of many Cups in a reading indicates a time during which the querent's actions will revolve around emotions. An Ace in a reading indicates new beginnings and is a number one. There is a focus on awakenings of new thoughts concerning inner desires. The presence of the Ace of Wands in a reading suggests that the querent is enjoying a time of pleasure and contentment. The querent will feel spiritually enlightened and at peace both with himself or herself but also with the world at large. The Ace of Cups represents joy, contentment, nourishment, abundance, fertility and spiritual fulfilment.

Reversed Meaning

When the Ace of Cups appears in the reversed position in a reading it represents instability, revolution and mutation. This could indicate that the querent is feeling anxious, which could result in instability, but the Ace of Wands is a generally favourable card and this should reassure the querent.

Special Consideration

As this is such a positive time for the querent it is a good time to explore new experiences. This card suggests that the querent will be successful in any pursuit.

Two of Cups

Pictorial Symbolism

There are two figures in the picture, one male and one female. Their posture and expression indicate that they are in love. They both hold a cup in their hands, and the male is reaching towards the female as if pledging his love. Above the figures is the caduceus of Hermes, between the great wings of which appears a lion's head. This is sign that has long been represented on this card in Tarot packs.

Divinatory Meaning

The presence of many Cups in a reading indicates a time during which the querent's actions will revolve around emotions. Twos in a reading indicate a period of gestation, of waiting and anticipation of great success in the future. There is a focus on relationships and matters of the heart. The presence of this card in a reading indicates the simple unity of two people in love. If the querent is forming a new relationship, this card's presence suggests that it will be extremely rewarding and successful. If the querent is in an ongoing relationship there will be renewed passion and communication. The Two of Cups in a reading represents love, passion, friendship, affinity, union, concord, sympathy and harmony.

Reversed Meaning

When the Two of Cups appears in the reversed position in a reading it represents almost the exact opposite – disharmony, separation, divorce and unsuccessful relationships. Partnerships could falter because too much energy is being put into them, creating an intense and suffocating relationship.

Special Consideration
The querent may find love with someone he or she had not previously thought of in a romantic way – it is important to keep an open mind and to be open to possibilities.

Three of Cups

Pictorial Symbolism

Three figures, all female, are standing in a close circle.
Each holds a cup and raises it upwards as if making a pledge.

The figures are standing in a garden, surrounded by plants and flowers. Their faces show joy and determination.

Divinatory Meaning

The presence of many Cups in a reading indicates a time during which the querent's actions will revolve around emotions. Threes in a reading suggest that more than one person is involved and can also suggest that there could be a period of suspended activity before future successes are realised. There is a focus on acceptance both of oneself and of others. The presence of the Three of Cups in a reading indicates that any problems that have arisen in the past will be resolved and the querent will be free to celebrate. The Three of Cups represents perfection, merriment, victory, fulfilment, solace and healing. The querent may receive some good news at this time.

Reversed Meaning

When the Three of Cups appears in the reversed position in a reading it represents excessive physical enjoyment on the part of the querent.

Special Consideration

If the querent has experienced difficult relations with another in the past, this would be a good time to clear the air. The querent should accept the positive traits and strengths of others as well as his or her own.

Four
of Cups

Pictorial Symbolism

The picture shows a young man seated under a tree. Before him are three cups that he is contemplating. To his right an arm issuing from a cloud is offering him another cup. It is clear from his expression and posture that he is discontented with his environment and he is not readily accepting the offer of another cup.

Divinatory Meaning

The presence of many Cups in a reading indicates a time during which the querent's actions will revolve around emotions. Fours in a reading indicate the realisation of one's goals. There is a focus on blended pleasure and weariness. The querent may be feeling anxious about an offer that has been made, and there may be doubts about the repercussions of accepting it. The querent will need to contemplate the benefits and risks – it would be better to err on the side of caution. The Four of Cups represents weariness, compromise, anxiety, mistrust and hesitation.

Reversed Meaning

When the Four of Cups appears in the reversed position in a reading it represents novelty, new relations, new instructions and possibilities. This clearly indicates that the querent will experience new beginnings.

Special Consideration

The querent should not give in to anxieties and difficulties in the present. The future will hold new opportunities and successes.

Five of Cups

Pictorial Symbolism

In the centre of the picture there is a figure dressed in a dark cloak. The figure is looking to his side, where three cups lie having been tipped over and their contents spilled on the ground around them. Behind him two cups remain upright. In the distance there is a bridge leading to a small settlement.

Divinatory Meaning

The presence of many Cups in a reading indicates a time during which the querent's actions will revolve around emotions. Fives in a reading indicate a time of changes and of ups and downs. There is a focus on loss. The querent may experience problems in a relationship. This card is frequently associated with marital difficulties and divorce. The querent may receive an inheritance, but this will bring little pleasure. The Five of Cups in a reading represents bitterness, frustration, inheritance, regret and depression.

Reversed Meaning

When the Five of Cups appears in the reversed position in a reading it represents news, alliances, affinity, ancestry, return and hope. The querent may hear news that an old friend will soon return.

Special Consideration

In time the bitterness that the querent is feeling will pass, and feelings of contentment and happiness will return. The querent should consider his or her reasons for these negative feelings and try to establish a positive goal or desire.

Six of Cups

Pictorial Symbolism

The picture shows two children standing on the outskirts of a settlement. One child holds a cup filled with flowers and the other is smiling up at him. There are five more cups filled with flowers around them. There are two interpretations of this scene. One is that it represents new experiences and the other is that it depicts a scene of things that are in the past, such as childhood.

Divinatory Meaning

The presence of many Cups in a reading indicates a time during which the querent's actions will revolve around emotions. Sixes in a reading indicate adaptability and the ability to change during difficult times. There is a focus on new environments and nostalgia. The changes that may occur in the querent's life may not have manifested themselves yet as this card indicates that the changes are in very early stages. The querent may meet up with old friends and enjoy reminiscing about the past together. The Six of Cups represents childhood, happiness, enjoyment, new environments, new employment and memories of the past.

Reversed Meaning

When the Six of Cups appears in the reversed position in a reading it represents the future, renewal and living in the past. This card could indicate that the querent is finding it difficult to face the future and feels lacking in emotional strength.

Special Consideration

The querent will feel peaceful at this time and will enjoy life's simple pleasures. The querent may even experiment with arts and crafts and discover hidden talents.

Seven
of Cups

Pictorial Symbolism

The picture shows the figure of a man with his back turned. He is looking in wonder at a fantastic vision

before him. The vision consists of seven cups floating
on clouds. The seven cups hold various symbolic ob-
jects – a snake, a castle, a dragon-like creature, a bowl
of jewels, the head of a young man, a laurel wreath, and
a mysterious figure hidden by shrouds.

Divinatory Meaning

The presence of many Cups in a reading indicates a time
during which the querent's actions will revolve around
emotions. Sevens in a reading indicate a time of solitude and asking questions of oneself. There is a focus
on deception. The querent will be faced with an offer
that may seem too good to be true. It would be prudent
to delay making any firm decisions until it is easier to
see the truth – at this time the querent will find the truth
hard to find. The Seven of Cups represents fairy favours,
images of reflection, sentiment, imagination and little
achievement. The querent may find his or her senses
clouded by emotional ties and sentimental feelings.

Reversed Meaning

When the Seven of Cups appears in the reversed position in a reading it represents desire, will, determination and success. The querent may be filled with strong
emotions that help to achieve success. It is important to
remember that success is not everything and can lead to
spiritual poverty.

Special Consideration

The querent should not be disheartened by the delay in activities. It would be wise to use the time to reflect on the positive aspects that already exist in his or her life.

Eight of Cups

Pictorial Symbolism

The picture shows the figure of a man walking towards
a distant mountain range. His posture suggests that he

is feeling dejected and defeated. He is walking away from eight cups that he has previously been working with. He does not look back but seems to have cut all ties with his previous enterprise.

Divinatory Meaning

The presence of many Cups in a reading indicates emotions. Eights generally represent positive changes. There is a focus on the completion of events. The querent may have been caught up in events that have been complicated and costly. This card indicates that the querent has decided to move on and leave the past behind. He or she will cut all ties with the events and will not even give them a thought once they are in the past. The Eight of Cups in a reading represents the decline of a matter, slight consequences, withdrawal and abandonment.

Reversed Meaning

When the Eight of Cups appears in the reversed position in a reading it represents great joy, happiness, material success and feasting.

Special Consideration

Once the querent has made the decision to move on, his or her attention will turn to seeking happiness. The querent will feel a load has been lifted and will be filled with optimism, which is a good start when seeking happiness.

Nine of Cups

Pictorial Symbolism

In the centre of the picture there is the figure of a plump and happy man sitting on a bench. He has recently feasted to his heart's content, and he has an abundant stock of wine in the cups on the arched counter behind him. This scene sows security and contentment.

Divinatory Meaning

The presence of many Cups in a reading indicates a time during which the querent's actions will revolve around emotions. Nines in a reading indicate the completion of events. There is a focus on harmony and balance. This is a positive card to draw in a reading as it indicates that the querent is overwhelmed by happiness on all levels. It could be that an enterprise undertaken has been successful . The Nine of Cups in a reading represents concord, contentment, victory, success, harmony, satisfaction and advantage.

Reversed Meaning

When the Nine of Cups appears in the reversed position in a reading it represents mistakes, imperfections, vanity and lack of humility. This card indicates that the querent may have been selfish and careless in victory, which led to mistakes being made.

Special Consideration

The querent should make the most of this very positive time and use his or her good fortune to help others whose

fortunes have not been so good. Generosity and kind-
ness bring their own rewards.

Ten
of Cups

Pictorial Symbolism

Across the top of the picture there is a row of cups forming a rainbow. Beneath the rays of the rainbow stand two figures in an embrace, each with an arm outstretched in wonder at the vision. It would seem that the two figures are husband and wife and the parents of the two children to their right. These children are unaware of the vision but are obviously happy as they hold hands and dance. In the distance the family home can be seen on a hill.

Divinatory Meaning

The presence of many Cups in a reading indicates a time during which the querent's actions will revolve around emotions. Ones in a reading $(1 + 0 = 1)$ indicate new beginnings and change. There is a focus on relationships. The querent will find that at this time relationships are harmonious and pleasurable. The querent may also feel a desire to be more involved in his or her home life and the community. The Ten of Cups in a reading represents contentment, repose of the entire heart, perfection, human love, friendship, family and home.

Reversed Meaning

When the Ten of Cups appears in the reversed position in a reading it represents conflict, broken relationships, a lack of harmony and false promises. The querent should not give in to the negative qualities of this card and should try to be strong in the face of adversity.

Special Consideration

This is a very strong card to be present in a reading and
its meaning will not be detracted from by other cards.
The querent should use this positive time to benefit those
he or she loves and cares for.

Page of Cups

PAGE of CUPS.

Pictorial Symbolism

In the centre of the picture there stands the figure of a
young page who is dressed in fine clothes. In his right

hand he holds a cup. From the cup a fish is rising to look at him. The page looks back at the fish with an expression of contemplation and intensity.

Divinatory Meaning

The presence of many Cups in a reading indicates a time during which the querent's actions will revolve around emotions. The Page of Cups is associated with the astrological sign of Pisces. There is a focus on news and business. The querent may hear some significant news, perhaps about the expansion of a business or a proposal of marriage. This news may come from someone who is gentle and artistic but who can surprisingly show courage and valour in times of need. The Page of Cups in a reading represents news, message, application, reflection, meditation and business issues.

Reversed Meaning

When the Page of Cups appears in the reversed position in a reading it represents seduction, deception, artifice, distractions and attachment. The querent may find himself or herself being seduced by fanciful ideas and false promises.

Special Consideration

The querent should be wary of accepting proposals too readily. He or she should assess what the heart truly desires and decide if he or she is ready for a significant change. There will be further opportunities in the future and if the time is not right now the querent should let this opportunity pass by.

Knight of Cups

KNIGHT of CUPS.

Pictorial Symbolism

A figure on horseback is seen riding through a dramatic
landscape. The figure is of a man dressed in armour, wear-

ing a winged helmet. He is sitting very straight in his saddle and in his right hand he holds out a cup. His manner is one of quiet grace rather than war, despite his attire.

Divinatory Meaning
The presence of many Cups in a reading indicates a time during which the querent's actions will revolve around emotions. The presence of a knight in a reading indicates that a stagnant situation will soon change. There is a focus on imagination and inspiration. The querent may be approached by a messenger bringing news that will have a powerful effect on his or her imagination. The querent may be overcome by strong emotions of passion and excitement. The Knight of Cups in a reading represents an invitation, arrival, approach, a messenger, propositions, enticements and imagination.

Reversed Meaning
When the Knight of Cups appears in the reversed position in a reading it represents trickery, artifice, subtlety, swindling, duplicity and fraud. The querent may be targeted by a character with much charisma.

Special Consideration
The querent should beware because the intentions of this character are to do the querent harm and should take care that his or her emotions do not overrule common sense.

Queen of Cups

QUEEN of CUPS.

Pictorial Symbolism

In the centre of the picture there is the figure of a majestic woman. She is seated on an elaborate throne that is resting on a small island in the sea. In her hands she holds an equally elaborate cup that is symmetrically designed, showing great balance. The woman is beautiful and has a dreamlike expression on her face as she looks at the cup. It is as if she can see a vision in the cup.

Divinatory Meaning

The presence of many Cups in a reading indicates a time during which the querent's actions will revolve around emotions. The Queen of Cups is associated with the astrological sign of Scorpio. There is a focus on development. The querent will enjoy the company of others at this time. The presence of this card indicates that the querent's relationships are strong and pleasurable. The Queen of Cups in a reading represents goodness, honesty, devotion, success, happiness, pleasure, wisdom, virtue and intelligence. The querent may well encounter a wise and loving woman who will be influential.

Reversed Meaning

When the Queen of Cups appears in the reversed position in a reading it represents deception, lack of trust, dishonour and falseness. The querent should exercise caution if he or she meets a woman who is apparently distinguished and popular as this woman could be untrustworthy and not all that she seems.

Special Consideration

This is a positive time for the querent and an excellent opportunity to strengthen relationships. At this time the querent will be feeling full of wisdom and should share his or her knowledge and experiences with others.

King of Cups

KING of CUPS.

Pictorial Symbolism

In the centre of the picture there sits the figure of a regal man on a throne. In his left hand he holds a short sceptre and in his right a great cup. The throne on which he sits is set upon the sea. On one side of him a ship is making its voyage and on the other side a fish is leaping. The implication is that the Sign of the Cup naturally refers to water, which appears in all the court cards.

Divinatory Meaning

The presence of many Cups in a reading indicates a time during which the querent's actions will revolve around emotions. The King of Cups is associated with the astrological sign of Cancer. There is a focus on business matters. The querent may well encounter a man who promises to be helpful in a business matter, and this could prove to be true. However, the querent should stay involved in the matter as the man may lose interest and enthusiasm towards the end, at which point the querent will need to step in. The King of Cups in a reading represents business, responsibility, creative intelligence, law and divinity.

Reversed Meaning

When the King of Cups appears in the reversed position in a reading it represents dishonesty, a double-dealing man, roguery, exaction, injustice, vice, scandal and considerable loss. If this card appears in a reading the querent would be well advised not to become involved in any new ventures with an unknown man.

Special Consideration
The querent may encounter a man of religious beliefs who may arouse the querent's interest in spiritual development.

Ace
of Swords

Pictorial Symbolism

The scene shows a rugged landscape above which a hand
issues from a cloud. The hand grasps a sword, the point

of which is encircled by a crown. From the crown plants are trailing. The way that the sword is being held, so upright and still, shows strength and triumph.

Divinatory Meaning

If a reading contains many Swords, it indicates a time of great activity in the querent's life. When an ace is drawn in a reading it is an indication of new beginnings as it is a number one card. There is a focus on critical and potentially volatile situations. The querent may well find himself or herself in the position of having to take action or make a decision under stressful circumstances. It is important for the querent to attempt to keep emotions balanced in order to make the correct decision. The Ace of Swords in a reading represents triumph, the excessive degree in everything, conquest and forceful emotions.

Reversed Meaning

When the Ace of Swords appears in the reversed position in a reading it represents disaster, destruction, excessive use of negative forces and hate triumphing over love. This card indicates that the balance of strong emotions has tipped strongly towards the negative, which is creating disastrous situations. The querent should try to stop the downward spiral and try to regain a balance of emotions.

Special Consideration

Once the querent has achieved a balance of emotions, he or she will go on to triumph and will enjoy success.

Two of Swords

Pictorial Symbolism

There is a figure of a young woman sitting on a stool with her back to the ocean. The woman is wearing a blindfold and has two swords held crossed across her chest. She wears a calm expression on her face and gives an impression of balance.

Divinatory Meaning

If a reading contains many Swords, it indicates a time of great activity in the querent's life. Twos in a reading indicate a period of gestation, of waiting and anticipation of great success in the future. There is a focus on negotiations. If the querent has been involved in a dispute with a friend or acquaintance, the presence of this card indicates that an amicable solution will be reached, with both parties feeling positive and glad that the dispute is over. The Two of Swords in a reading represents courage, friendship, concord, affection, communication, compromise and harmony.

Reversed Meaning

When the Two of Swords appears in the reversed position in a reading it represents duplicity, falsehood, disloyalty and release. The querent should be wary of another who seeks a compromise but is unwilling to make concessions.

Special Consideration

The key to achieving a satisfactory compromise is open and honest communication. The querent should not let previous bitterness influence the communication. Once a compromise has been reached the querent should feel a sense of achievement at having been open-minded and considerate of others.

Three
of Swords

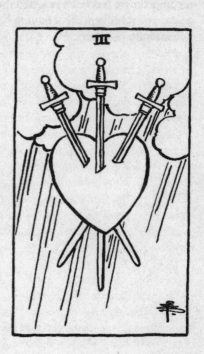

Pictorial Symbolism

In the centre of the picture is a heart being pierced by
three swords. Behind the pierced heart are clouds and

rain. This card obviously symbolises sadness and heart-ache.

Divinatory Meaning

If a reading contains many Swords, it indicates a time of great activity in the querent's life. Threes in a reading suggest that more than one person is involved and also suggest that there will be a period of suspended activity before future successes are realised. There is a focus on separations and loss. Unfortunately this card indicates an unhappy time in the querent's life. The querent may well be experiencing difficulties in a relationship that could lead to separation. The cause of these difficulties is likely to be jealousy or interference by another party. The Three of Swords in a reading represents removal, absence, delay, division, rupture, depression and separation.

Reversed Meaning

When the Three of Swords appears in the reversed position in a reading it represents mental alienation, error, loss, distraction, disorder and confusion. The querent may find that he or she is becoming obsessed with negative experiences that are happening in the present and are denying previous happier times. The querent should step back from the situation and try to be more objective.

Special Consideration

The querent should try not to be too depressed by the negative events taking place. They will not last forever and once this difficult time is over he or she will feel a sense of release and wellbeing.

Four of Swords

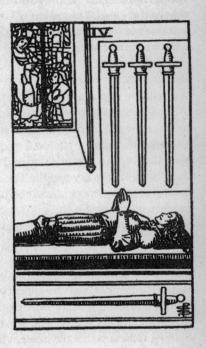

Pictorial Symbolism

A knight can be seen lying upon his tomb while holding his hands in prayer. There is a stained-glass window above him, suggesting that he is in a holy place. Three swords are suspended above him and another lies at the side of the tomb. The knight is taking time to reflect in solitude but he will not remain in retreat. His dress suggests a moment of respite rather than a permanent state.

Divinatory Meaning

If a reading contains many Swords, it indicates a time of great activity in the querent's life. Fours in a reading indicate the realisation of one's goals. There is a focus on retreat and contemplation. The querent has previously been involved in complicated and highly charged situations involving many people. The querent now feels the need for solitude and a chance to meditate and be at peace with himself or herself. The Four of Swords in a reading represents vigilance, retreat, solitude, repose and exile.

Reversed Meaning

When the Four of Swords appears in the reversed position in a reading it represents isolation, loneliness, detachment and seclusion. The presence of this card in a reading indicates that the querent has been in retreat for too long or at the wrong time, and has become cut off and may have missed out on opportunities as a result. The querent should make attempts to re-integrate and socialise.

Special Consideration

The querent will feel truly at peace during this time of solitude and may find spiritual enrichment through meditation and reading. However, the querent should be wary of cutting ties with friends and should not isolate himself or herself.

Five of Swords

Pictorial Symbolism

The scene is set under stormy skies. In the foreground a disdainful man looks after two rejected and defeated figures, his face shows at their loss. The man carries two swords on his left shoulder and another in his right hand. At his feet lie the swords of the retreating figures. The man is the master in possession of the field.

Divinatory Meaning

If a reading contains many Swords, it indicates a time of great activity in the querent's life. Fives in a reading indicate a time of changes and of ups and downs. There is a focus on bitterness and frustration. The querent may have been involved in a conflict that has brought to light an unpleasant and devious side of his or her character. Such is the nature of this type of conflict that no party will win or triumph as the parties involved will sink to any level to try to win. The result will be unhappiness and grief for both parties. The Five of Swords in a reading represents degradation, destruction, dishonour, infamy, loss and devastation.

Reversed Meaning

When the Five of Swords appears in the reversed position in a reading it represents uncertainty, weakness, humiliation and mortification. The querent will be antagonised by a rival, and gossip and rumours will spread round the querent's friends. The querent should be strong at this time and should not feel pity for the rival as it will be interpreted as weakness.

Special Consideration

The querent should be aware of the negative aspects of his or her character that are surfacing and should try to redress the balance by acting positively and not giving in to the negative desires. Using positive affirmations in meditation may help the querent to feel more positive.

Six
of Swords

Pictorial Symbolism

A ferryman is carrying his passengers to a distant shore.
In his boat are a mother and child and six swords so his

load is not heavy. The water is calm and the crossing is causing the ferryman little cause for exertion.

Divinatory Meaning

If a reading contains many Swords, it indicates a time of great activity in the querent's life. Sixes in a reading indicate adaptability and the ability to change in times of difficulty. There is a focus on obstacles overcome. The querent may have been struggling with difficult situations recently, but this card indicates that the querent has managed to achieve a balance and to create order in his or her life. The querent may well feel in need of a break or holiday, and this card indicates that he or she will travel, possibly over water. The Six of Swords in a reading represents journeys, routes, success, resolution of difficulties, peace and calm.

Reversed Meaning

When the Six of Swords appears in the reversed position in a reading it represents regrets, disappointments, disillusionment, travel and journey. The querent may well decide to go away for a break in order to get over disappointments. The querent will benefit from the break and will return with a lighter heart.

Special Consideration

The querent should recognise the new skills and

strengths that were developed during the time of difficulties that he or she experienced. These skills and strengths will have made the querent a stronger person, and in future times of difficulty he or she will be able to draw on these new strengths.

Seven of Swords

Pictorial Symbolism

A figure can be seen to be stepping carefully away from
a camp. In his arms he carries five swords. Behind him

a further two swords are planted in the ground. The figure looks over his shoulder to make sure that no one sees him as he makes his exit.

Divinatory Meaning

If a reading contains many Swords, it indicates a time of great activity in the querent's life. Sevens in a reading represent a time of solitude and of asking questions of oneself. There is a focus on adjustments and ill-conceived plans. The querent may be involved in a scheme that is moderately successful. Another person may approach the querent with ideas of how to improve the venture. The querent should be wary of fanciful promises and should look carefully at the situation before making adjustments. The querent needs to remain concentrated at this time and should keep distractions to a minimum. The Seven of Swords in a reading represents design, attempts, wishes, hopes, confidence, quarrelling, a plan that may fail, and annoyance.

Reversed Meaning

When the Seven of Swords appears in the reversed position in a reading it represents confusion, bad timing, loss of concentration and defeat. This card indicates that during a struggle the querent chose to relax at the wrong time, and this resulted in the other party taking advantage, leaving the querent confused.

Special Consideration

If the plan does not work out the querent should not look to place the blame on others but should look to himself or herself for reasons for the failure. This card indicates that the most likely cause of failure is hasty actions and lack of concentration.

Eight of Swords

Pictorial Symbolism

A figure of a young woman bound and blindfolded
stands on the shore. She is surrounded by eight swords

planted in the sand. Behind her a castle stands on a hill. The woman is not bound in such a way that she could never hope to be free, and there is a feeling that this is a scene of temporary duration rather than of irretrievable bondage.

Divinatory Meaning

If a reading contains many Swords, it indicates a time of great activity in the querent's life. Eights in a reading are generally positive and represent positive changes. There is a focus on imprisonment. The querent may be feeling trapped by a situation in his or her life, and is unable to express his or her feelings. The querent may become involved in several unsuccessful ventures in an attempt to gain freedom. The Eight of Swords in a reading represents crisis, conflict, censure and entrapment.

Reversed Meaning

When the Eight of Swords appears in the reversed position in a reading it represents disquiet, difficulty, opposition, treachery and hopelessness. The querent may be feeling weighed down by the confines of his or her situation and be unable to see any reason to be hopeful. The querent should be strong and try to fight for his or her liberty.

Special Consideration

Although the querent is feeling trapped by his or her

situation, the mind is free and full of activity. The querent should use this time to reflect on how the situation came about and how he or she will act once it is over. Once the querent is free of his or her prison, he or she will feel a new sense of determination and strength.

Nine of Swords

Pictorial Symbolism

The figure of a woman, disturbed from sleep by a terrible sorrow, is sitting up in bed with her head held in her hands. Above her nine swords are hanging. The darkness of the room and the posture of the woman show that this is a card that represents desolation.

Divinatory Meaning

If a reading contains many Swords, it indicates a time of great activity in the querent's life. Nines in a reading indicate the completion of events. There is a focus on suffering and anxiety. This card is often associated with miscarriages and accidents, and the unbearable mental torment that follows such events. The querent may well be feeling very low at this time and may find it difficult to keep the strength needed to carry on. The Nine of Swords in a reading represents failure, miscarriage, delay, deception, disappointment, despair and death. This is an introspective time for the querent, and others who wish to help will find they get little response.

Reversed Meaning

When the Nine of Swords appears in the reversed position in a reading it represents doubt, suspicion, imprisonment, fear, guilt and shame. The querent may be depressed because he or she is feeling guilty about something that has happened. This depression could affect the querent's physical wellbeing, and he or she should try to seek help for the depression before he or she becomes very ill.

Special Consideration

As the querent is feeling very low at this time, he or she has little energy so the best way to cope is to let fate run its course without fighting it. Eventually this depression will lift and happiness will re-enter the querent's life.

Ten
of Swords

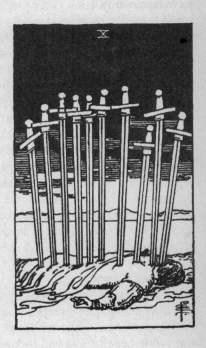

Pictorial Symbolism
Under a dark sky a prostrate figure pierced by ten swords
lies on a bleak landscape. The figure has been stabbed

in the back, so the attack was unexpected and could well have been a trap.

Divinatory Meaning

If a reading contains many Swords, it indicates a time of great activity in the querent's life. Ones in a reading (10 - 1 + 0 = 1) indicate new beginnings and changes. There is a focus on failure and destruction. Despite the violent scene depicted on the card, this card does not necessarily represent a violent attack. It does suggest, however, that the querent's enemies have weapons that could be used to cause the querent harm. The presence of this card indicates that the destructive situation that the querent is involved in has reached a climax, and in the near future the querent will be able to think more clearly. The Ten of Swords in a reading represents pain, affliction, tears, sadness and desolation.

Reversed Meaning

When the Ten of Swords appears in the reversed position in a reading it represents advantage, profit, success, favour, power and authority. However, these will all be short-term benefits and will lack permanence.

Special Consideration

The querent should look carefully at the other cards to get an impression of which area of his or her life will be effected by this card. It is important for the querent to stay strong as this card represents the end of a negative situation and the beginning of change. The querent will experience a clarity of thought as a result of the recent traumas.

Page
of Swords

PAGE of SWORDS.

Pictorial Symbolism

A lithe, active figure holds a sword upright in both hands
while in the act of swift walking. He is passing over

rugged land, and about his way the clouds are gathered wildly. He is alert and lithe, looking this way and that, as if an unexpected enemy might appear at any moment.

Divinatory Meaning

If a reading contains many Swords, it indicates a time of great activity in the querent's life. The Page of Swords is associated with the astrological sign of Taurus. There is a focus on perception. The presence of the card indicates that the querent is involved in a secretive situation that requires skills of observation, devotion and subtlety. The Page of Swords in a reading represents authority, overseeing, secret service, vigilance, spying, agility and examination.

Reversed Meaning

When the Page of Swords appears in the reversed position in a reading it represents underhanded deeds, deceit, deviousness and callousness. The card in this position suggests that the secretive person's actions have become malicious. As a result bad feelings will surface and may result in a violent confrontation.

Special Consideration

The querent should be aware that secretiveness can lead to confusion and lack of trust. The querent should not leave close friends in the dark as they may wrongly interpret the situation and reach their own conclusions.

Knight of Swords

KNIGHT of SWORDS.

Pictorial Symbolism

The knight can be seen to be riding in full course, as if scattering his enemies. He holds his sword high as he charges forth, and his face shows that he intends to attack. However, there is also something rather romantic about the figure. He is depicted as a stereotypical hero of chivalry.

Divinatory Meaning

If a reading contains many Swords, it indicates a time of great activity in the querent's life. The presence of a knight in a reading indicates that a stagnant situation will soon change. There is a focus on reckless actions. The querent may find himself or herself involved with a person who acts impulsively and whose thoughts are erratic. This person could either be an enemy of the querent or a loyal friend whose intention is to act in the querent's favour. The Knight of Swords in a reading represents skill, bravery, capacity, defence, address, wrath, war, destruction, opposition, resistance and ruin.

Reversed Meaning

When the Knight of Swords appears in the reversed position in a reading it represents imprudence, incapacity, extravagance and indiscretion. This suggests that actions are poorly thought out and that the querent has become too indulgent. It is necessary to step back from the situation and to think objectively in order to regain balance.

Special Consideration

The querent should pay careful consideration to the other cards in the reading as they hold the key as to which area of the querent's life will be affected. The querent should be wary of indulging in impulsive and erratic actions and should try to create balance by acting in a very stable manner.

Queen of Swords

QUEEN of SWORDS.

Pictorial Symbolism

The queen sits on her throne on a hill. Her right hand raises her weapon vertically and the hilt rests on the arm of her royal chair. Her left hand is extended with her hand raised. Her countenance is severe and chastened, suggesting that she is familiar with sorrow. This figure gives no indication of mercy or compassion. Although she is a queen holding a large sword the figure does not symbolise power.

Divinatory Meaning

If a reading contains many Swords, it indicates a time of great activity in the querent's life. The Queen of Swords is associated with the astrological sign of Virgo. There is a focus on sadness but also perception. The Queen of Swords in a reading represents widowhood, female sadness, embarrassment, absence, sterility, mourning, privation, separation and intelligence. The querent may be involved with a woman who has experienced sorrow and has become dispassionate but quick-witted as a result. This woman can act quickly and severely.

Reversed Meaning

When the Queen of Swords appears in the reversed position it represents malice, bigotry, artifice, prudery and deceit. This card indicates that a woman, possibly the querent, has become embittered as a result of a sorrowful experience. This woman has a sharp tongue and can cause distress to others by making stinging comments.

Special Consideration
The querent should attempt to help the sorrowful woman
come to terms with her misery before it turns to bitterness. The querent should highlight the positives that still
exist in life and the potential joys that the future holds.
It is important, however, to respect and acknowledge
the pain and sorrow that the woman has experienced.

King of Swords

KING of SWORDS.

Pictorial Symbolism

The king is a commanding figure as he sits in judgment
on his throne, holding an unsheathed sword. He is a con-

fident figure and his gaze is penetrating. He is a powerful individual with the ability to make important decisions.

Divinatory Meaning

If a reading contains many Swords, it indicates a time of great activity in the querent's life. The King of Swords is associated with the astrological sign of Libra. There is a focus on decisive actions. The King of Swords in a reading represents power, command, authority, militant intelligence, law and enforcement. This card indicates that the querent is, or is involved with, someone who is detached and determined in thought and action.

Reversed Meaning

When the King of Swords appears in the reversed position in a reading it represents cruelty, perversity, barbarity and evil intent. This card indicates that the querent is, or is involved with, a man who is tyrannical in his behaviour, a man who has become completely detached from human suffering and enjoys imposing his will. Although this man may appear calm and confident, his inner feelings are of great unhappiness.

Special Consideration

The querent should endeavour to ensure that the man does not become extreme in his detachment and cold-heartedness. The querent should highlight the consequences for others of actions that may benefit the man.

Ace of Pentacles

Pictorial Symbolism

A hand issues forth from a cloud with a pentacle cupped in the palm. The hand is suspended above a garden in bloom. There is a path from the garden to the mountains in the distance.

Divinatory Meaning

If a reading contains many Pentacles, it signifies that the querent will feel that situations are taking form. When an ace is drawn in a reading it is an indication of a new beginning as it is a number one card. There is a focus on the realisation of goals. The querent may have been working towards a goal for some time, and the presence of this card suggests that the hard work has paid off. The rewards may be seen in a business venture or personal relationships. It may even signify the birth of a child. The Ace of Pentacles in a reading represents perfect contentment, ecstasy, gold, intelligence and joy.

Reversed Meaning

When the Ace of Pentacles appears in the reversed position in a reading it represents the evil side of wealth, preoccupation with material assets, prosperity and comfortable material conditions. The querent may have become spiritually impoverished as a result of material self-indulgence.

Special Consideration

This is a very positive time for the querent. However,

the querent should be wary of being carried away by the luxuries of material wealth. It is always important to remember that there are others who lack such riches.

Two of Pentacles

Pictorial Symbolism

The figure of a young man can be seen to be dancing while balancing a pentacle in each hand. The two pentacles are linked by an endless cord that is like the number eight reversed. Behind the figure, boats are sailing over seas with prominent waves and troughs.

Divinatory Meaning

If a reading contains many Pentacles, it signifies that the querent will feel that situations are taking form. Twos in a reading indicate a period of gestation, of waiting and anticipation of great success in the future. There is a focus on the need for balance. This card in a reading suggests that situations in the querent's life could develop either positively or negatively, so the querent needs to juggle his or her affairs to keep the balance. There is the possibility that the querent may travel at this time. The Two of Pentacles in a reading represents gaiety, recreation, news, obstacles, agitation, trouble and embroilment.

Reversed Meaning

When the two of Pentacles appears in the reversed position in a reading it represents enforced gaiety, simulated enjoyment, a lack of willpower and disharmony. The querent's mind is preoccupied with a previous event. It is necessary for the querent to resolve this situation before he or she will feel truly joyful.

Special Consideration

If the querent is able to keep his or her affairs balanced,

this will be a very positive time, and there will be a great many rewards. The querent will feel in control and euphoric.

Three of Pentacles

Pictorial Symbolism

Three figures can be seen standing in a monastery. One
is a sculptor at work as the other two watch him at his

craft. Above them all, three pentacles are forming a design at the top of a pillar.

Divinatory Meaning

If a reading contains many Pentacles, it signifies that the querent will feel that situations are taking form. Threes in a reading suggest that more than one person is involved and can also suggest that there will be a period of suspended activity before future successes are realised. There is a focus on the recognition of skills and hard work. The querent may find that employers or potential employers have taken note of his or her abilities and quality of work. The querent may be called on to work on a project that will benefit from his or her skills. The Three of Pentacles in a reading represents trade, skilled labour, renown, glory and recognition.

Reversed Meaning

When the Three of Pentacles appears in the reversed position in a reading it represents mediocrity, pettiness, weakness, lack of skill and inefficiency. The querent may have made grand plans regarding a work venture but later lost interest and enthusiasm, resulting in sloppy work. It may be best to cut one's losses if renewed motivation can not be found.

Special Consideration

The querent will get a great amount of personal satisfaction from the success of the venture and from recognition from others. The spiritual rewards will be great though the material gain may be less than expected.

Four of Pentacles

Pictorial Symbolism

A crowned figure sits on a stool in front of a town. There is one pentacle balanced on his crown, one held in his arms and another one under each foot.

Divinatory Meaning

If a reading contains many Pentacles, it signifies that the querent will feel that situations are taking form. Fours in a reading indicate the realisation of one's goals. There is a focus on material wealth. The querent may receive a large sum of money that will ensure his or her financial security. This money may be an inheritance or a golden handshake from an employer. The Four of Pentacles in a reading represents gifts, legacies, inheritance and wealth.

Reversed Meaning

When the Four of Pentacles appears in the reversed position in a reading it represents suspense, obstacles, delay, opposition and loss. Others have become jealous of the querent's wealth and are plotting to create obstacles.

Special Consideration

This card indicates that the querent will enjoy a rewarding time financially at this time. In order to gain this material wealth, however, it seems that the querent may experience a loss. Inheritance may be gained through the death of a relative or close friend, and a golden handshake would mean the end of a time of employment. Such losses may leave the querent feeling alone and lost, and financial security is sometimes cold comfort.

Five of Pentacles

Pictorial Symbolism

Two downtrodden figures pass a lighted stained-glass
window with five pentacles forming the design. One of

the figures would appear to be a leper as he has a bell around his neck. Both would appear to be destitute as they are both walking through the snow in ragged clothes.

Divinatory Meaning

If a reading contains many Pentacles, it signifies that the querent will feel that situations are taking form. Fives in a reading indicate a time of changes and of ups and downs. There is a focus on financial or personal difficulties. The querent may experience problems at work that can cause concerns regarding financial security. Problems in a relationship may arise from arguments about money or because infidelity is suspected. The Five of Pentacles in a reading represents poverty, emotional problems, loneliness, troubled thoughts and financial insecurity.

Reversed Meaning

When the Five of Pentacles appears in the reversed position in a reading it represents disorder, chaos, ruin, discord and loss. The querent may feel that circumstances are outside his or her control, and the querent's health may begin to suffer as a result. The querent should look for ways to salvage what can be saved and then cut his or her losses and start anew.

Special Consideration

The querent should examine his or her situation closely and decide if a solution is likely to present itself in the near future. If not, the best course of action may well be to bow out of the situation in the early stages rather than become involved in a draining struggle. Once definite action has been taken the querent will be free to mourn and grieve and then begin to heal and feel better.

Six of Pentacles

Pictorial Symbolism

A man dressed in the clothes of a merchant is weighing his money in a pair of scales that he holds in one hand.

With the other hand he is distributing money to the needy and distressed. Above him six pentacles are floating in the sky. The scene shows that the merchant is successful but also has goodness in his heart.

Divinatory Meaning

If a reading contains many Pentacles, it signifies that the querent will feel that situations are taking form. Sixes in a reading indicate adaptability and the ability to make changes in times of difficulty. There is a focus on accomplishments and rewards. The querent may have been involved in a business venture that has proved to be a wise investment as financial rewards will be great. The querent will have achieved success through hard work and the success is deserved. The querent will be considerate of others, especially those who helped along the way, and will become known for his or her generosity. The Six of Pentacles in a reading represents presents, gifts, gratification, prosperity and attention.

Reversed Meaning

When the Six of Pentacles appears in the reversed position in a reading it represents envy, jealousy, desire, illusion and selfishness. The querent may be jealous of another's wealth and may live more extravagantly than his or her means allow.

Special Consideration
The querent may well find himself or herself in a very influential and powerful position, which will be demanding but also rewarding. The querent will also feel rewards from being able to be generous and charitable.

Seven of Pentacles

Pictorial Symbolism

A young man leaning on his staff looks intently at seven
pentacles attached to a clump of greenery to his right.

He looks at them as if assessing the gains of his labour.

Divinatory Meaning

If a reading contains many Pentacles, it signifies that the querent will feel that situations are taking form. Sevens in a reading indicate a time of solitude and asking questions of oneself. There is a focus on limited successes. The querent may be involved in a venture that has little financial reward but serves to help a friend. The querent will be satisfied once the enterprise is concluded as a debt will have been repaid and a job will have been done well. The Seven of Pentacles in a reading represents business, limited success, hard work and favours returned.

Reversed Meaning

When the Seven of Pentacles appears in the reversed position in a reading it represents anxiety, impatience, disappointments and concerns regarding money. A friend may approach the querent for a financial loan. The querent may have doubts about the friend's intentions or ability to repay the loan. The querent should not give the loan if lack of repayment would cause him or her financial difficulties.

Special Consideration

The querent may have resigned himself or herself to the

fact that the project in which he or she is involved will be non-profitable, but it could be that a lack of vision is limiting the success. It is possible that with enthusiasm and hard work the venture could be more profitable than expected.

Eight of
Pentacles

Pictorial Symbolism

A sculptor is engraving pentacles on stone circles. He
displays the products of his hard work on the tree be-

side him. The sculptor is concentrating hard on his labour and is being very industrious as he has produced eight finished pieces of work.

Divinatory Meaning

If a reading contains many Pentacles, it signifies that the querent will feel that situations are taking form. Eights in a reading are generally very positive and represent positive changes. There is a focus on the building of foundations for future success. The querent will be justified in having high hopes for the future as present situations and ventures are going well and the outlook is good. The querent will have worked hard to create this state of affairs, and continued hard work will be required. The Eight of Pentacles in a reading represents work, employment, commission, craftsmanship, skill, business and a bright future.

Reversed Meaning

When the Eight of Pentacles appears in the reversed position in a reading it represents vanity, exaction, a lack of ambition, avarice and greed. The querent may desire financial rewards but lacks the skill and ambition at this time to achieve it. The querent should be wary of seeking dishonest means of finding financial success as it could lead to spiritual impoverishment if others suffer as a result.

Special Consideration

The querent should not lose interest or involvement in other areas of his or her life and should be wary of becoming obsessed with the venture. Friends and those close to the querent may start to feel unneeded and seek fulfilment elsewhere if they are neglected.

Nine of Pentacles

Pictorial Symbolism

A woman, with a bird upon her wrist stands amid a great
abundance of grapevines in the garden of a manor house.

It is a wide domain, suggesting plenty in all things. Possibly it is her own possession and testifies to material wellbeing. At her feet on one side six pentacles are balanced and three are balanced on the other side.

Divinatory Meaning

If a reading contains many Pentacles, it signifies that the querent will feel that situations are taking form. Nines in a reading indicate the completion of events. There is a focus on positive rewards. The querent may have been working on a venture alone. During this time the querent may have had to be self-sufficient and rely on inner strengths. This card suggests that the hard work will be paid off and will be recognised and rewarded. If the querent has recently heard of an inheritance it could well turn out to be of greater value than first thought. The Nine of Pentacles in a reading represents prudence, safety, success, accomplishment, discernment and certitude.

Reversed Meaning

When the Nine of Pentacles appears in the reversed position in a reading it represents roguery, deception, bad faith, danger and threats. The querent may be involved in the theft of a sum of money or the loan of money used for illegal gains.

Special Consideration

The querent will receive financial rewards, and these will bring pleasure. However, for the querent the real pleasure will come from knowing that he or she alone was responsible for the success, and the querent will be filled with a sense of self-worth.

Ten of Pentacles

Pictorial Symbolism

A man and a woman stand facing each other beneath an
archway that opens onto a settlement. The pair, possi-

bly husband and wife, are accompanied by a small child.
The child is watching intently as an elderly person, seated
in the foreground, is greeted by two dogs and is reaching out to pat one of the dogs.

Divinatory Meaning

If a reading contains many Pentacles, it signifies that the
querent will feel that situations are taking form. Ones in a
reading (1 + 0 = 1) indicate new beginnings and change.
There is a focus on family matters. The querent will find
that his or her home is the most powerful influence in his
or her life at this time. It could be that another member of
the querent's family is having a difficult time financially
and the querent is in a position to help out. The Ten of
Pentacles in a reading represents gain, riches, family matters, home and distribution of wealth.

Reversed Meaning

When the Ten of Pentacles appears in the reversed position in a reading it represents chance, fatality, loss and rob-
bery. The querent may experience a temporary setback.
Losses experienced at this time will be expected or minor.

Special Consideration

The querent now has the opportunity to repay his or her
family for all its support and love. The querent will be
able to show gratitude by sharing wealth and rewards.

Page of Pentacles

PAGE of PENTACLES.

Pictorial Symbolism

The figure of a young man stands in an open landscape.
His hands are raised and above them a pentacle hovers.

The man is gazing at the pentacle intently and is oblivious to all else.

Divinatory Meaning

If a reading contains many Pentacles, it signifies that the querent will feel that situations are taking form. The Page of Pentacles is associated with the astrological sign of Capricorn. There is a focus on study. If the querent has recently been studying for an examination the presence of this card in a reading suggests that the result will be favourable. This card indicates that the querent will receive some form of good news at this time. The Page of Pentacles in a reading represents application, study, scholarship, reflection, news and messages.

Reversed Meaning

When the Page of Pentacles appears in the reversed position in a reading it represents dissipation, concern, disappointment and rebellion. This could indicate that a young person in the querent's life has rejected study and caused disappointment.

Special Consideration

The querent will be rewarded for a period of study that required self-discipline and determination. The querent will feel proud of his or her efforts and will feel greater confidence in his or her abilities.

Knight of Pentacles

KNIGHT of PENTACLES.

Pictorial Symbolism

The knight rides on a slow, enduring and heavy horse.
Indeed, the knight could be said to resemble the horse

in many ways. He holds forth a pentacle but does not look at it or take joy from it.

Divinatory Meaning

If a reading contains many Pentacles, it signifies that the querent will feel that situations are taking form. The presence of a knight in a reading suggests that a stagnant situation will soon change. There is a focus on a hard-working character. The querent may be, or be involved with, a solid and trustworthy character who is keeping a venture going by doing hard work that is not always recognised or rewarded. The Knight of Pentacles represents patience, hard work, interest, responsibility and methodical work.

Reversed Meaning

When the Knight of Pentacles appears in the reversed position in a reading it represents inertia, idleness, stagnation, discouragement and carelessness. The querent or another may have an idea for a venture, but those approached for cooperation lack enthusiasm.

Special Consideration

The querent may benefit from the work and service of a solid man. The querent should appreciate his help and reward him justly. The character who is helping is likely to have a temper that is slow but once roused hard to cope with. The querent should be aware of this.

Queen of Pentacles

QUEEN of PENTACLES

Pictorial Symbolism

The queen sits on her throne surrounded by nature in full bloom. On her knee rests a pentacle, and she contemplates it and sees great visions in it. She is an intelligent woman with a great soul.

Divinatory Meaning

If a reading contains many Pentacles, it signifies that situations are taking form. The Queen of Pentacles is associated with the astrological sign of Aquarius. There is a focus on ambitions and aspirations. The querent may encounter a sensible woman who will prove to be helpful in a business matter. The woman will be intuitive about other people and will be able to identify their strengths and weaknesses. The Queen of Pentacles represents opulence, generosity, security, liberty and magnificence.

Reversed Meaning

When the Queen of Pentacles appears in the reversed position in a reading it represents evil, suspicion, suspense, fear and mistrust. The querent may encounter a woman who causes problems in the querent's social circle and arouses feelings of mistrust.

Special Consideration

Situations are going well for the querent at this time and will continue to do so. The querent should be thankful to the woman who is offering help in business matters but should not lose confidence in himself or herself and become reliant on her perception.

King of Pentacles

Pictorial Symbolism

The king sits on his elaborate throne. He is wearing robes
made from fancy, fine material and behind him is his

domain. His face shows courage but also a certain amount of lethargy.

Divinatory Meaning

If a reading contains many Pentacles, it signifies that the querent will feel that situations are taking form. The King of Pentacles is associated with the astrological sign of Gemini. There is a focus on financial success. The querent may encounter a man who is able to offer guidance and assistance in a financial matter. This man will be wise in business matters but lacking in social graces and an appreciation of the arts. The King of Pentacles in a reading represents valour, intelligence, business aptitude and mathematical gifts.

Reversed Meaning

When the King of Pentacles appears in the reversed position in a reading it represents vice, weakness, ugliness, perversity, corruption and peril. The querent may encounter a bitter man who seeks to cause others harm and misfortune.

Special Consideration

The querent may well have a great deal of respect for the man who shows such intelligence regarding business matters but should not try to be like him. The querent should recognise that the man lacks spiritual riches and leads quite a lonely life.

Glossary

cartomancy the art of telling fortunes by using cards.

court cards the Kings, Queens, Knights and Pages of the suits of the Minor Arcana.

Cups one of the suits of the Minor Arcana.

deck a pile of cards.

divination the act of predicting events.

divinator one who foretells events.

divinatory meaning the interpretation of individual cards and the possible implications for the querent.

Major Arcana the first twenty-two cards in a Tarot pack.

Minor Arcana the remaining fifty-six cards divided into four suits.

New Age   a movement or philosophy concerned with spiritual harmony and ecology.

occult   the supernatural.

pack   a set of cards.

Pentacles   one of the suits of the Minor Arcana.

pictorial   interpretations of Tarot cards based on

symbolism   the picture alone.

Querent   the person who seeks advice from the Tarot cards.

reading   the interpretation of a spread of Tarot cards.

significator   the card chosen to represent the querent or situation in question.

special consideration   further advice as to the best course of action relating to individual cards.

spread   the arrangement of Tarot cards in patterns that allow divination.

suit	one of the four sets in the Minor Arcana of a Tarot pack.
Swords	one of the suits of the Minor Arcana.
Wands	one of the suits of the Minor Arcana.